The Unive

Pathfinder

The Universal Gardens

**An introduction to the 30 day programmes
that will change your mind, body, spirit and life
through discovering your inner Universal Gardens**

**Written by Grace Brown
& designed by David Thorley**

www.TheUniversalGardens.com

Pathfinder

The Universal Gardens™ Copyright © 2012 by Universal Gardens Media Ltd.

Created and produced by Grace Brown & David Thorley
Edited by Paul Herrington

Images by Unholy Vault Designs at Shutterstock.com

Grace Brown and David Thorley have asserted their right to be identified as the authors of this Work in accordance with the Copyright, Designs and Patents Act 1988.

All rights reserved.

NO RESALE RIGHTS ARE ACCORDED WITH THE SALE OF THIS BOOK.

Reproduction, copying or any other form of use of the pieces contained within the book is STRICTLY FORBIDDEN with express permission from the author. If perjury is discovered the offenders will be prosecuted to the full extent of the law.
No part of this book may be used or reproduced in any manner whatsoever without written permission. This book may not be lent, resold, hired out or otherwise disposed of by way of trade in any form, binding or cover other that in which it is published, without the prior consent of the author. These rules have been established to protect the rights and ownership of the authors and to ensure that their work is upheld as their own.

LEGAL NOTICES AND DISCLAIMER

The following terms and conditions apply:

The views and opinions expressed are entirely those of the authors.

While all attempts have been made to verify information provided, neither the authors, nor any ancillary party, assumes any responsibility for errors, omissions or contradictory interpretation of the subject mater herein.

Any perceived slights of specific people or organisations are unintentional.

To the fullest extent permitted by applicable laws, in no event shall the authors, publisher, agents or suppliers be liable for damages of any kind or character, including without limitation any compensatory, incidental, direct, indirect, special, punitive or consequential damages, loss of use, loss of data, loss of income or profit, loss of or damage to property, claims of third parties or other losses of any kind or character, even if the authors of this book have been advised of the possibility of such damages or losses arising out of or in connection with the use of this book.

This book gives non-specific, general advice and should not be relied on as a substitute for proper medical consultation. The authors and publisher cannot accept responsibility for illness arising out of the failure to seek medical advice from a doctor.

ISBN 978-0-9570907-1-2

www.TheUniversalGardens.com

If one is the master of one thing and understands one thing well,
one has at the same time insight into
and understanding of many things.
Vincent Van Gogh

Contents

Introduction 8
The Gardens 22

Part One
Daily Life Changing Concepts

1 Energy 38
2 Direction 50
3 Emotional Guidance 68
4 Belief Systems 76
5 Layers 82
6 Intentions 84
7 Forgiveness 92
8 Affirmations 108
9 The Universal Laws 126
10 What you resist, persists 168
11 Gratitude 176
12 De-cluttering your life 182
13 Chakras 202

Contents

Part Two
The Universal Gardens

14 The Universal Garden Wheel 228
15 The Money Garden 246
16 The Love Garden 262
17 The Goals and Desires Garden 274
18 The Guardian Angel Garden 288
19 The Healing Garden 296
20 The Dreams and Aspirations Garden 310
21 The Angel Garden 324
22 The Forgiveness Garden 338
23 The Releasing and Letting Go Garden 352
24 The Fountain of Youth Garden 362
25 The Crystal Garden 374
26 The Gratitude Garden 388
27 Conclusion 400

INTRODUCTION

You are a vibrational energy being that is constantly in a state of creation and you are connected to everyone and everything in this bountiful universe. You are interconnected. You create with your thought energy and when this thought energy is turbo charged with emotions of joy and gratitude you will be creating the things you love and the life you desire.

If your thoughts are focused on worry, unhappiness or lacking and turbo charged with negative emotions then sadly all you are doing is creating more of the things you do not wish for.

It is human nature for many to unconsciously focus their thought energy on the things they do not wish for because these are habits; people are so used to the negative thoughts, because the negative thoughts have made themselves at home within their mind. Thoughts are energy and our inner chatter is words strung together.

Many of these words will be negative "I don't want to be poor", firstly there are many words that the universe does not understand for instance the word 'don't', when you say" I don't desire to be poor, the universe interprets as "I desire to be poor", so this book will assist with positive as opposed to negative wording.

You are creating your own path for life moment by moment whether you are consciously aware of it or not. You have choices and what you choose is entirely up to you. This book will guide you to make the right choices, those being the choices that will bring you joy and happiness. This book offers diverse tools and techniques and information about not only changing how you think and feel but also about cleansing and healing your mind, body, spirit, chakras and subtle layers.

There is also something that is indicative to our emotions on a daily basis and that is the moon. No, I am not going all weird on you; I am simply offering vital information regarding the moon and your emotions. The moon has a great influence on your emotions and when you discover how to work side by side with the influences of the moon you will make the choices that are right for you.

There is a section about the moon and its gravitational pull on your emotions and if you follow the tools and techniques for embracing the beautiful moon you will be astonished by the results.

Key Point...

Throughout this book I will be referring to Source energy.

It is the Source energy that we are all connected to; it is the creative energy that includes everyone and everything in this universe.

I have been working with Source energy for many years, though at first it took a while to connect, however when I eventually did I discovered how easy the state of pure blessedness is to achieve.

Once you have digested the relevant information and begin using the specific tools and techniques you will be able to enter into your very own state of blessedness.

The Source energy can be manipulated to form whatever we desire in our lives.

We are always each and every one of us manipulating our energy moment by moment whether you are consciously or unconsciously aware of this fact.

> We are universal artists creating our masterpiece of life.

You will learn to walk the walk and talk the talk
of who you truly wish to be.

You will discover how to move into the state of pure blessedness and enjoy feeling blessed moment by moment.

A state of blessedness is working with Source energy and acknowledging pure gratitude for everything and everyone that encompasses your life. This state of blessedness is achieved by understanding everything about you and your personal aura.

You will discover the energy layers and chakras within the aura. By gaining an understanding of these layers and chakras you will be able to enhance all levels of your life, mind, body and spirit.

Disease begins in the subtle energy layers. The etheric layer for instance is the layer closest to your physical body and any type of illness manifests in the etheric layer before it is apparent in the physical body. Illness lies dormant in the etheric until it is triggered and then it will transmute into the physical body.

The objective is to heal any imbalances with the subtle layers before they become established within the physical body and more complex to cure. Your thought energy and emotions will play a huge roll in affecting the condition of these bodies and have an intense impact on your health

It is vitally important that you aware of how your mind, body and spirit can be affected if it is not given the correct care and attention.

The energy has to flow freely and unobstructed, you have to be in the flow, flowing freely and easily. Being in the flow is all about feeling your way with non resistance. Non resistance is not going against something.

When I am flowing I feel amazing.
I have butterflies in my tummy.
I smile a lot and feel joyfully blessed.

If you have a problem in your life and you resist it by either not facing up to it or burying it, you are giving more power to the problem, it takes over you. Because you are resisting you are surrounding the problem with further negative energy. When you resist you are persisting the problem and it becomes stronger and over facing.

I feel very fortunate as I am in the flow most of the time; this is because twice a day I engage myself in one of the gardens.

You can be in the flow too if you allow how you are feeling to be your emotional guidance, guiding you to your desires. It is always about how you feel; feelings are the key to the vibrations you are offering.

The tools and techniques in this book will help you to recognise when you are flowing freely and easily.

You will know when you are free flowing. If your life is a breeze and you feel good, your home and work life is great and your friendships are happy ones and you are experiencing financial freedom then yes you are in the flow.

If on the other hand you are up against it where work is not great or your home life is not hunky dory and nothing seems to be going well for you and you do not feel good...then sadly you are not flowing freely.

The Universe can bring to you everything that you desire all you have to do is feel your way by releasing any resistance.

The universe is certainly not stopping you from achieving your dreams you are. The universe is kind and generous and wishes to give you everything you wish for, the universe is not holding back your desires you are.

The reason you are not in the flow is down to the beliefs that you hold that have been ingrained in you from birth by your parents, elders, and teachers. It is your beliefs that stop you being in the flow.

You are no different from anyone else apart from your belief system. If you see yourself as beautiful and with the golden thread of unconditional love running through you that is what you will be. If you see yourself as unattractive and unlovable then that is what you will be. Whatever you feel about yourself is exactly what you will be.

You may believe that you have to work hard to earn your money, this is not so. This is fear based beliefs that have been fed to you and not true. If you wish to work yourself into the ground then do so; however all you are doing is using up precious energy.

There is much fear in the world which is sad, there ought to be mountains of love not fear. You can move mountains with love, fear keeps you stuck in a rut.

Many religions are fear based. So many people believe that they are meant to suffer as it is a kind of punishment for something they may have done in the past, or desiring money means you are bad, these fears are so wrong.

There are so many God fearing people around and yet God is full of love and compassion for all and would not wish people to be fearful, God would wish for us all to discover the golden thread of unconditional love running through everyone and everything.

What the Universal Garden Series is all about

> *Focus on the journey, not the destination.*
> *Joy is found not in finishing an activity but in doing it.*
> Greg Anderson

The Universal Garden Series viewpoint is one of health and wellbeing. In simple terms, it is a holistic system which guides you to living a healthier and more balanced lifestyle. Each individual Garden recognises that you are a unique individual and focuses on tools and techniques to restore balance and harmony to your individual make-up.

The wisdom of 'The Universal Garden Series' guides and encourages you to take responsibility for your own mental, emotional and spiritual well-being; all of which have a big impact on your health, adapting your lifestyle accordingly so that you can enjoy living in harmony, living life to the full.

This pathfinder book is designed to help you to discover how you can truly heal your life and decide which 'Universal Garden' is going to benefit you the most at this point in your life. Each garden is inspiring, motivating and has the power to provoke great changes in how you think, feel and act.

Each Garden has the power to break down old beliefs and inject wisdom into your life, helping you to discover that you have the power within you to enhance your life.

Key Point...

Throughout the book I will explain the deeper meanings of each individual Garden with detailed examples and different exercises for you to follow. It will be entirely up to you which garden path you go down. You will find this information valuable and positive in helping you to discover and explore not only your journey in life, but 'The Universal Garden Series' as well. Whichever Garden you choose will help you to attain your goals and desires, as well as creating a life full of optimistic, rewarding, loving and blessed relationships.

Finding your true dreams and desires can be a long, drawn out and sometimes wearisome search for the keys to your own personal path. Those keys will unlock the riches housed within you. Unlocking the riches within is one of the most important parts of achieving your dreams and desires; gathering health, wealth, abundance, success and discovering strong personal relationships.

You will eventually understand that it is your personal beliefs and emotions that direct and constrain you, forming your personal world and the world as a collective. You will learn about the two aspects of the mind and the influences each of them have on your day to day life.

Every single thought that you think (positive or negative) flows through your body, affecting your inner and outer world. So if your thoughts are positive and constructive then excellent, if they are bordering towards the negative side then sadly things will not be great for you.

The pathfinder handbook will help you to discover the 'Universal Garden Series' and show you how to take control of your health and wellbeing with thoughts and feelings that will raise your vibratory level to one of vitality and delight.

The Pathfinder is a valuable tool to discover your own unique way on this journey of life.

> Some things have to be believed to be seen.
>
> Ralph Hodgson

KEEPING A POSITIVE JOURNAL

You will require a journal, a nice one if possible as you will be writing in it every day. Since I began journalling in 1999 I have written and filled over forty six journals and when I look at what I have written I find it quite amazing how my life has transformed into what I actually wrote and wished for.

When you are buying your journal ensure that it is nice and something you would desire to write in on a daily basis. The secret to success in life is to keep a journal. A journal should be written in everyday to capture your gratefulness and your dreams and desires.

Writing a journal provides the opportunity to review what you wish for.

The success seed is planted in the mind. Writing a journal is crucial to your success seed sprouting. Personal development and future success should be written in your journal. Journalling is always in the positive and in the present tense "I am grateful for everyone and everything in my life, thank you".

Always take your journal with you everywhere you go. The Universal Garden DayBook is excellent as it is a diary, journal and self help book all rolled into one and excellent visually too.

Discover your own style of writing and review what you have written daily. Reviewing your journal on a daily basis ensures that you are keeping your focus on your desires.

> Journalling can be useful for your success in moving on in your life.
>
> Grace Brown

THE UNIVERSAL GARDEN SERIES WILL HELP YOU TO...

Take action. For every action there is a reaction

Become a magnet for success

Manifest money

Discover your Angels and Guardian Angels

Release the past and move onto an amazing future!

Heal your mind, body and spirit

Discover the right direction for you RIGHT NOW!

Determine your goals and complete them

Consider your relationship with you, your family, partners and friends

Discover how to become a conscious creator

Make conscious choices about a successful career

Discover the golden thread of love within you

Release outworn beliefs

An old belief is like an old shoe.
We so value its comfort that we fail
to notice the hole in it.

Robert Brault

THE UNIVERSAL GARDEN SERIES

WELCOME TO THE FIRST 12 GARDENS...

The Money Garden

The Love Garden

The Goals and Desires Garden

The Guardian Angel Garden

The Healing Garden

The Dreams and Aspirations Garden

The Angel Garden

The Forgiveness Garden

The Releasing and Letting Go Garden

The Fountain of Youth Garden

The Crystal Garden

The Gratitude Garden

If you want to make your dreams come true, the first thing you have to do is wake up.

J.M. Power

THE MONEY GARDEN

Relates to your current financial status,
effectively moving you to a state of financial freedom

THE LOVE GARDEN

Relates to the love of you, your spouse,
family and friends.
If you are lacking in this area,
this garden will help you to discover
the golden thread of love.

The Goals and Desires Garden

Relates to you discovering what your
true goals and desires are in life;
as well as showing you how to achieve them.

THE GUARDIAN ANGEL GARDEN

Relates to you discovering your personal
Guardian Angel that has been with you on
your journey from birth until your death.
This garden will help you to identify and
make contact with your Angel;
enhancing not only your life but your Guardian Angels too.

THE HEALING GARDEN

Relates to the health and well being of your life.
You will find that true healing occurs
at source level in this garden.

THE DREAMS AND ASPIRATIONS GARDEN

Relates to your dreams and aspirations,
this garden will show you not just how to raise them
but also how to achieve them.

THE ANGELS GARDEN

Relates to your Angelic realm,
this Garden will show you how to open the door
to communicating with The Angels;
enabling you to start on a magnificent
journey of enlightenment.

THE FORGIVENESS GARDEN

Relates to you removing the shackles of un-forgiveness, enabling you to live a life of freedom and joy

THE RELEASING AND LETTING GO GARDEN

Relates to you releasing and letting go of all negativity from your mind, body and soul; allowing you to live a healthy, happy and abundant life.

THE FOUNTAIN OF YOUTH GARDEN

Relates to you transforming your mind, body and spirit by rejuvenating your energy on all levels. In this garden you will learn how to enhance your youthfulness and revive your spiritual essence.

THE CRYSTAL GARDEN

Relates to you bringing harmony to your mind,
body and spirit through the use of crystals.
Working on the subtle layers and chakras
you will discover your connection to Mother Earth;
learning to channel unwanted energies
back to her for recycling.

THE GRATITUDE GARDEN

Relates to having or not having gratitude in your life.
It will show you how to be grateful for everyone
and everything in your life;
which then brings you more things to be grateful for.

PART ONE
DAILY, LIFE CHANGING CONCEPTS

In Part One of the Universal Gardens Pathfinder you will find a wide range of techniques that will enable you to change your life.

In Part Two, you will be shown twelve Universal Gardens, a magical place for you to visit whenever you want, to improve your life in any particular direction.

The Universal Garden concept is unique - not only does it give you the ideas and concepts you need, but it also provides a wide range of practical exercises that you can incorporate into your daily life.

Then you can begin to enter the particular Universal Gardens that you are attracted to.

This makes the Universal Gardens a very powerful way to break those old habits and forge a new path in your life.

Everything you will need is here in the Pathfinder.

This book was designed as a reference, so after you have familiarised yourself with the main concepts, study the chapters you feel you need.

Then begin!

Always remember to keep this Pathfinder handy, so you can re-read and re-visit these powerful concepts.

Please use the exercises and charts to help you create your new future, they are real tools that will give you guidance and stability through a period of transition.

CHAPTER ONE

THE ESSENCE OF EVERYTHING IS ENERGY

Everything and everyone vibrates at different frequencies, each vibrational frequency is unique to that person or object. It is vitally important that you are aware of your vibratory frequency through your conscious understanding. You need to be in the present moment and be constantly aware of how you are feeling.

If you do not feel quite right or you feel out of sync then you know you are going in the wrong direction and giving off the wrong signal or vibration which is or will deeply affect how you feel emotionally and in turn will affect your emotional and mental state as well as affecting your environment.

You require that inner knowing that you are off course with your signals so that you can change how you are currently vibrating to set you back on course. For this to happen you have to reclaim your personal power by changing your thought processing, releasing outdated beliefs.

The first thing that you should know about energy is that it cannot be created or destroyed, it simply changes form.

We are all masters of our universe and have personal power over our lives.

THE MIND IS AN AMAZING THING AND CAN PRODUCE NEGATIVE OR POSITIVE ENERGY VIBRATIONS THROUGH THE THOUGHTS THAT WE THINK...

Your thoughts are energy and your thoughts, feelings and actions have their own particular rate of vibration.

This means that you are constructing your life minute by minute, either consciously or unconsciously which is quite scary really.

Each vibration resonates with one and the same frequency (like attracts like).

We are vibratory beings offering a vibratory signal, and also receiving signals so we are not only a transmitter of energy we are also a receiver of energy.

This of course means that what you are offering as your personal vibration you are attracting into your life a similar vibration.

The result being a magnetism of conditions, people, and opportunities that resonate with your key vibratory frequency.

Things, people, circumstances, events and situations resonate with your vibratory signal and find you.

ENERGY AND VIBRATIONS

This is a great analogy of how energy vibrates. If you can imagine a desk fan with its rotors, now imagine it turned off, you can see the rotor blades very clearly and distinctly.

If you were to turn on the fan to its lowest speed, you can still see the rotor blades turning.

If you were to turn the fan to medium speed the fan rotors will become increasingly harder to see, (you know they are still there but they are not easy to see).

So if it were turned to high speed you definitely would not see the rotor blades turning, in fact it looks as though all of the rotor blades have disappeared that is because they are invisible to the eye.

Now you certainly would not presume that the rotors have disappeared simply because we do not see them whizzing around.

This analogy of the fan is exactly the same as your energy system and how we all vibrate as humans.

THOUGHTS AND THEIR VIBRATIONS

We are now going to look at the valuable mind tool that we all possess. To move on and enhance every part of your life there are certain things you need to know about your conscious and subconscious mind. This is very important information and once absorbed and put into practice you can begin to change your life beyond comprehension.

Once you have an understanding of the subconscious mind, and your ability to control its function, you will be creating more of what you desire in life, eradicating things that you do not wish for. You will become the 'Master of your Universe' enabling you to begin to intentionally create the life you have always dreamed of.

All truly wise thoughts
have been thought already,
thousands of times;
but to make them truly ours,
we must think them over again honestly,
till they take firm root
in our personal experience.

Johann Wolfgang von Goethe

SUBCONSCIOUS AND CONSCIOUS MIND

Everyone's mind is unique; there are two individual sides of the mind the first being your conscious mind and the other being your subconscious mind. (There is also the pre-conscious mind, however to keep it simple and easy for you to understand we will concentrate only on the conscious and subconscious mind)

Let us look at the connection between the two aspects of the mind, the conscious and subconscious mind.

Sigmund Freud a Viennese physician and the founder of Psychoanalysis proposed the iceberg metaphor likening the two aspects of the mind to an iceberg. Imagine the iceberg is your mind.

The conscious mind is the tip of the iceberg, the part you see. The subconscious mind, which is the main and most controlling part, lies unseen below the water controlling the iceberg.

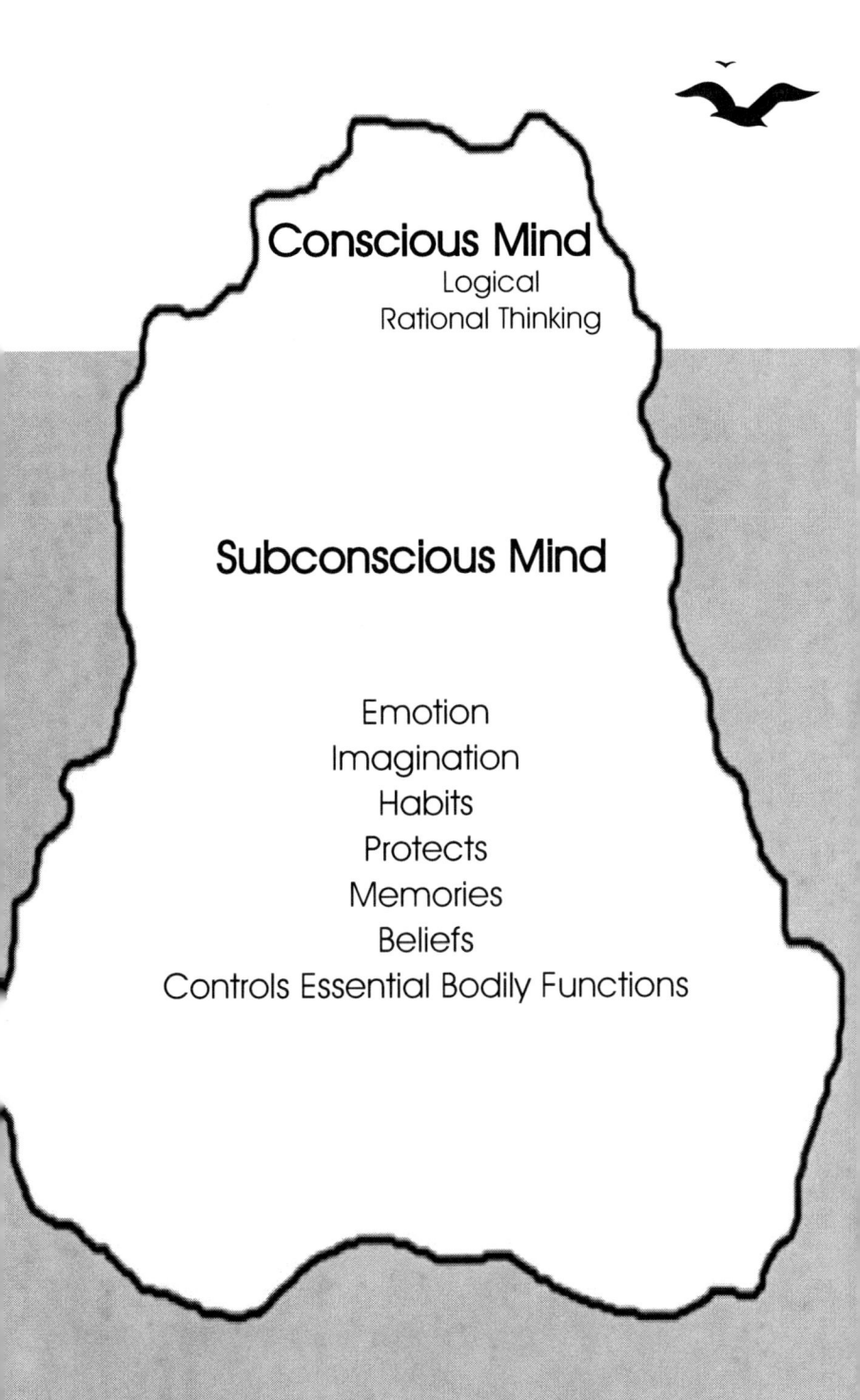

THE UNIVERSAL GARDEN SERIES WILL SHOW YOU...

Your conscious mind directs your subconscious mind
by giving it orders.
Your subconscious mind dutifully accepts the orders given
based on what your conscious mind accepts as true.

Your conscious mind gathers together all of the information
through your five senses (sight, smell, taste, hearing and touch)
where you perceive them as your personal reality or experiences.

Your subconscious mind then stores the realities or experiences.

The submerged part of the iceberg that is unseen is very deep
and is far greater in size than the visual tip of the iceberg.
Similarly the subconscious mind has far greater influence
than the conscious mind.

There is no doubting the remarkable control
that is in action below that tip of the iceberg.
The iceberg is no different to the subconscious in action.
The subconscious mind regulates the beating of your heart,
your breathing, digestion and your blood flow
(these are just a few to mention).

It is with your conscious mind which you speak and think.

It is your subconscious that is your personal genie,
and this you must always remember.

'The Universal Garden Series' ensures that you never forget
the power of your personal genie.

'The Universal Garden Series' guides you to cultivate new ways of
dictating to it, because your subconscious acts upon your orders.

> **It is psychological law that whatever we desire to accomplish we must impress upon the subjective or subconscious mind.**
> Orison Swett Marden

> Any thought that is passed on to the subconscious often enough and convincingly enough is finally accepted.
>
> Robert Collier

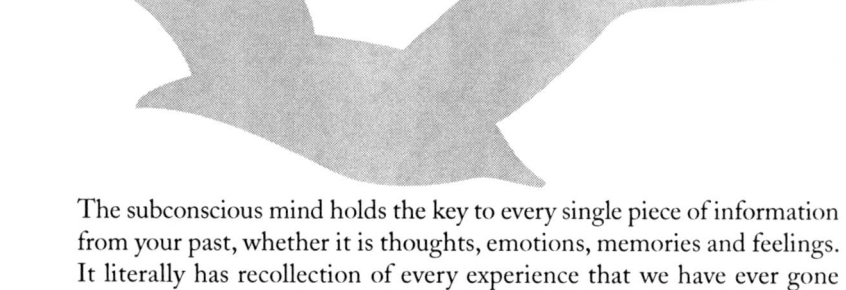

The subconscious mind holds the key to every single piece of information from your past, whether it is thoughts, emotions, memories and feelings. It literally has recollection of every experience that we have ever gone through that is why it is called the storehouse of our memories and emotions.

Have you ever heard a particular song or something on the TV, or radio that you are trying to recall a particular piece of information? Your subconscious mind is aware and ready to help you to recall the relevant information.

Now, it may not happen instantly, particularly if it is a very old deeply seated piece of information, however the subconscious mind will carry out the mission of locating it through its memory storehouse for the relevant information.

You will know the moment the subconscious mind has the information as it will make you aware of the answer the moment it has been recovered. You could be in the midst of doing something quite unrelated, like cooking dinner, taking a shower or literally anything when the answer is revealed to you.

KEY POINTS TO REMEMBER REGARDING THE SUBCONSCIOUS MIND...

The subconscious mind is always the victor;
it will always overrule logical thoughts

The subconscious mind is the seat of your emotions

Your subconscious mind never makes judgements
of your thoughts or feelings or actions

Every single feeling of emotion (good or not so good)
is stored within the subconscious realm

Everything you experience is stored in the cellular structure
of your body too. (See cellular memory section below)

Familiar events will be felt immediately within
the cellular memory of your body

You can have anything you desire, anything at all.
The secret is to lift the veil of limiting beliefs
that you have ingrained within you

Your subconscious will always be protective towards you.
It will always restrain painful memories until it feels
that you are ready to feel and heal them

When you have a belief that you will never be slim,
your subconscious will do everything in its power to execute
that your belief comes true for you by making you over weight.
The same applies to money, if you think that you will always be
on the breadline then you always will be.
(Your wish is my command master said the faithful genie)

The subconscious will respond all thoughts and feelings
whether of love or fear, so choose your thoughts wisely

Each individual 'Universal Garden Handbook'
works with the subconscious mind
and with conscious thought processing.

To see the full range, do not forget to visit
the Universal Gardens website!

**Sign up for your free newsletter
and to see the latest news at
www.TheUniversalGardens.com**

Key Point...

If you really desire to change your life, only you can do this.

You can do it by shifting the programming of your subconscious mind from the negative to positive.

This is not an easy feat though because by consciously deciding to change how you think will not carry any weight with your subconscious programming. 'The winner takes it all and the winner is your subconscious mind always'.

In order of shifting your thought processing you have to play tricks on your subconscious mind. Your emotions are habituated because of how you have been programmed; this is your belief system. To change your life you have to change your beliefs by assuming a new belief system.

Whichever Universal Garden you decide to go into will be for a minimum of thirty days because it takes twenty one days to break a habit and thirty days to form a new one.

So please do not think that you can decide to do something consciously because you cannot do it single handed.

Your new beliefs must be realistic and be meaningful for your conscious and subconscious mind to take on board.

CHAPTER TWO

> A man sooner or later discovers
> that he is the master-gardener of his soul,
> the director of his life.
>
> James Allen

DID YOU KNOW YOU ARE THE AUTHOR, PRODUCER, EDITOR, ACTOR AND DIRECTOR OF YOUR LIFE...

You are the author, producer, editor, actor and director of your life and you direct your life with your thoughts and feelings. Thoughts are energy. A feeling is something you feel within your body's awareness to something or it can be a feeling linked with something emotional, such as happiness or sadness.

Emotions are also feelings or reactions to something. Everyone has feelings moment by moment; you cannot help having feelings, they are part of everyone. You encounter an array of feelings all day long as different things occur whether you are consciously or unconsciously aware.

When your thoughts are charged with emotion they are a powerful driving force for attracting positive and negative circumstances. It is through your thoughts and emotions that you experience your reality.

If you tend to focus more on the negative than the positive please do not think there is anything wrong with you, it is merely a habit. Habits can be changed just the same as thoughts can. Habits creep up on you. When you learn to walk as a child, your brain will make associations that generate neurological activity pathways. When you habitually stand up and walk, your brain learns the pattern of walking and sets up a pathway.

This new pathway is simple to follow and now becomes a habit where it can be accessed easily and processed. You can now see that once a pathway is formed it is not easy to eliminate, which is why working in one of The Universal Gardens is extremely beneficial in eliminating old habits and negative self talk.

If you would like to change an outdated habit for a new one, this can actually be quite simple when you use the tools and techniques of your chosen Garden. Going into your chosen garden on a daily basis, you can indoctrinate a new habit within 30 days. That is, on the proviso that, your new habit is not opposing your old habit.

When your thoughts are charged with emotional energy the effects can be immense as long as your thoughts are good and productive, if they are not then the effects can be debilitating. It is how you are feeling that establishes your personal vibrational frequency. Happiness or sadness is always created within and mirrored into your reality.

When things are going well and things are tickety boo you will experience good strong feelings, the good feelings emit a high frequency of vibration into the universe which will be matched and then energy vibrations of a similar frequency will be sent back into your reality.

Now if on the other hand you are emitting vibrations that are of a low frequency this is because you are not feeling good or you are worried, therefore your lower vibrational frequency will once again be matched and mirrored back into your reality bringing to you more of not feeling good or worrying more about situations in your life.

During these times when things go wrong try to see the wrongs as learning lessons in life, see them as stepping stones to your success, chances to stretch and grow.

How to use your energy...

Your life is an energetic cycle!

Raise your vibrational offering by focusing on what you desire

When you place your focus on what you do not desire
you will receive more of what you do not desire

Being consciously aware of how you are feeling
determines your vibrational state

The Universe responds to your vibration and reflects it back to you

You can make a decision to be happy and fulfilled in life so do it NOW

When you focus on the negative you will be in resistance,
this resistance will repel abundance

> Have you ever wondered what your subconscious mind looks like? Well today, I can show you.
> David Icke

ENERGY AND EMOTIONS

Vibrations are the key to everything in life. Recognising that everything has a vibrational frequency means you can begin to monitor your own vibrational frequency.

We live in a universal sea of energy where nothing is solid, everything is made up of atomic particles vibrating at such a high frequency that they appear as solid to the naked eye, a chair for example. Because we have a limited sense of sight we cannot see the vibration of the particles, we just see a physical chair. The wavelength and frequency of light we see, also influences the colour we see.

The essence of everything is energy, you and me; absolutely everything is energy whether animate or inanimate. Thoughts are vibratory and unseen, it is our thoughts that permeate the environment, pulsating and travelling through time and space. We immerse thought energy of those around us, and are constantly interacting unconsciously with each other. If the energies we are immersing are positive that is excellent, however if they border on the more negative side then these will affect your health and well-being.

Before we move onto the individual 'Universal Gardens' there are things that you will need to be aware of and understand, in order to move forward in your life in an unobstructed way. I will not baffle you with science; I will merely give you some basic life changing information that if recognised and used in your day-to-day living will not only change and enhance your life it will enhance your total well-being and of those around you.

I will be discussing energy, sometimes I may talk about stuck, congested, or stagnant energy. This stuck, congested or stagnant energy isn't really stuck, as energy is always in motion, it is basically emotions, traumas and feelings that have not been processed or released. Emotions play an integral role within our physical and mental health. Emotions are connected to your thoughts, feelings, and actions and are always intermingling, influencing different characteristics of you.

If all of your thoughts and emotions are all good vibrations then those vibrations will determine what your future experiences will be because of the Law of Attraction. That which you give your attention to, will be drawn into your life experience

DID YOU KNOW THAT MOST PEOPLE THINK AROUND 60,000 THOUGHTS A DAY?

Each thought carries an energetic vibration. You have approximately 60,000 thoughts a day, and around 80% of those thoughts are negative and many of those thoughts are repeated numerous times on a daily basis.

You are often thinking about what is going to happen in the future, or perhaps reliving the past, fixating on the past or the future will be the foundation of the life that you are creating for yourself.

You have to understand that your repetitive thoughts and the emotional reactions to those thoughts are customary to your way of thinking. Thoughts that are firmly ingrained on your subconscious mind are there because of the attention you have shown them and are now firmly stuck in place by the intensity of your emotional reaction to them.

Your negative thought patterns will cause mayhem in your life. Habitually thinking the same thoughts will become "real" in your mind, and therefore become your beliefs.

Because you do not know any different and are happy to remain in your comfort zone you continue repeating the same thoughts.

Having constructive and optimistic thoughts, good intentions and actions will not create negative results; however by engaging in negative thinking and unconstructive actions certainly will not create positive results.

If you can tip the scales
and go for 75%
of positive thoughts,
you will be a force
to be reckoned with
and an amazing manifestor!

All that we are is the result of what we have thought.
Buddha

SOWING THE SEEDS OF GOOD THINKING

If you can try to be consciously aware of your thoughts and recognise how many times you repeat the same thoughts and be conscious of them being positive or negative, by being consciously aware you will realise that you are continually repeating the same thoughts over and over again.

Negative thoughts are draining. Unless your mind is engaged with something, it will automatically go on auto-pilot and connect to thoughts that you have a strong emotional response to.

We all become so involved on focusing on the past or the future that we are not aware what's going on right under our nose. When you allow your mind to run riot the thoughts you are focusing on are sticking to your mind like glue and in turn are mirrored into your reality. Your mind is an amazing tool, learning how to use it consciously will have dramatic affect on your day to day living!

Your thoughts are an essential part of what you are if you learn to train your mind and stop repeating the same old thoughts you will release the genie-magic of your mind. This takes practice, work and definitely dedication. If you can try for 21 days to focus 25% of your thoughts on the things you would love to have in your life like, love, joy, happiness, financial freedom and many different dreams and desires, you will be tipping the scales to more positive outcomes in life.

If you can focus 50% of your thoughts on the positive then you are halfway to achieving your dreams and desires, which is amazing.

TRY THE FOLLOWING TIPS...

Being present in the moment is your main point of power,
so be there as often as possible

Set good strong positive intentions every day!

Show gratitude for everyone and everything in your life

Smile as much as you can, smile, smile and smile some more!!!

Be nice to yourself and treat others as
you would like to be treated yourself

Plant your seeds with faith for expansion and opportunities in life

Use the affirmation "I am present in this moment
and consciously aware of everyone and everything"

Be around positive people as much as possible

Spend your time and energy on things that bring you joy and happiness

Laugh a lot, laughter is infectious and good for the soul

Being Connected

Every one of us in the universe is connected because we are all inter-connected with the energy and vibrations of the universe. The universe is omnipresent and omnipotent. There is nowhere the universe is not present, it is everywhere. Have you heard "I feel as if I am carrying the weight of the world on my shoulders" you are literally, the universe will always be there sitting on your shoulders, helping you to fly like a bird or weigh you down.

Look at yourself as a piece of a jigsaw with energy; that is a piece of the whole universal jigsaw with your shape, size and colour. In the light of things we are all energy pieces of the universal jigsaw and therefore we all make up the universal jigsaw to make it complete.

We play a very important role in the jigsaw as a whole because without you the jigsaw would not be complete, it would not be whole.

The jigsaw will only be complete if others add their piece of the jigsaw. Look at it this way we are all here for a reason. We all have a purpose in life, we are here to make a difference to the world and it is our contribution that will make a difference. We have to wake up and smell the roses and start to fulfil our purpose or life contract.

Finding Your True Motivation

Be aware that whatever you are saying, thinking or doing in your life, you are in fact making a difference; your vibration (whether good or not too good) is out there looking to resonate with energies similar to your own. It means that you attract what you are focusing on within your life by your subconscious and conscious mind and the law of attraction.

Now if you are a negative unforgiving person well sadly the people that you attract into your life will be negative and unforgiving. You are always making your mark in life because you are a part of something very significant.

Try not to unconsciously go through life, live your life consciously and use your thoughts to your advantage by allowing them to be good healthy thoughts. Think, health, success, love and allow your thoughts to be intense and positive and therefore you will connect with the same by attraction.

Always remember that energy cannot be created or destroyed.

It simply moves form.

EMOTIONS AND THEIR WARNING SYSTEM

Emotions are our warning system, our emotional guidance system. We are walking, talking emotional energy beings with built in emotional warning systems. It is our emotional guidance that is letting us know if we are on the right track, and what is happening around us. Too often because we really do not wish to deal with things that upset us we consciously block out the emotional traumas and upsets.

With any kind of trauma or upset we tend to put them on the back burner, always thinking I will deal with this later, and sadly the backburner is your subconscious mind. It is your subconscious mind, your memory storehouse that already has all of your unprocessed emotions and traumas already stored within its cellular memory. It is your conscious mind that you think with and whatever you mainly think about drops down into your subconscious mind, which then comes into fruition through your reality.

WHAT IS CELLULAR MEMORY?

In brief according to some theorists cellular memory means that the brain is not the only organ in the body that stores memories or personality individualities. Memory can form in other systems in the body and can be stored in cells and organs such as the Lungs and heart. The cells of the body retain memories independently from the brain.

E.g. someone may have a heart transplant and are totally unaware of the age and sex of the donor. The person that received the transplant after a while may find that they are yearning certain foods or drinks, or they may suddenly decide to take up an activity that is totally out of character for them. This is cellular memory!

> Be not afraid of life.
> Believe that life is worth living,
> and your belief will help create the fact.
> — Henry James

FLIGHT OR FIGHT RESPONSE

This next piece of information is something that everyone should know and understand, as it can literally help you to understand your emotions and what is happening to you during distress.

There is a part of the brain housed within the temporal lobe called amygdala that controls fear and anxiety amongst other emotions. It is a part of the brain that is connected to memory and helps the brain learn and retain information. This part of the brain is responsible for the processing of emotions such as panic and dread, happiness and anger.

The amygdala is also influential as to what memories are stored in your brain. The emotional response of trauma or shock means your body will go into fight or flight mode secreting nor-adrenaline hormones and cortisol. Whenever the memory of an event is recalled or recognised as distressing or uncomfortable, your cellular memory reacts and then literally overflows your body with these hormones, therefore leaving your immune system tired and openly susceptible to attack.

Amygdala controls: memory, emotional reactions, autonomic responses associated with fear, stimulation-arousal, and the secretion of hormones.

During situations when your fight or flight response is activated, chemicals, nor-adrenaline, adrenaline and cortisol are released into your bloodstream. Due to the chemical release your body will experience a sequence of changes with your heart rate, blood pressure and breathing.

BODY SIGNS...

Your responsiveness intensifies.

Your impulses accelerate.

Your sweat glands open, making the skin look pale and damp.

Your pain awareness reduces.

Your pupils dilate to see more clearly, even in the dark.

Your sight becomes rapid.

Your immune system is fired up.

You scan and explore your environment,
"Seeking your enemy."

You are prepared physically and psychologically
for your response of fight or flight.

Once your fight or flight system is triggered, everything in your environment you perceive as a danger to your survival. Your rational mind goes into "fight" mode. Your free will is eliminated. You are not thinking clearly you see everything as a danger to your survival. In your state you see everyone and everything as a potential threat.

FIGHT OR FLIGHT...

Your fear will be exaggerated.

You are not thinking straight.

Everything you see and feel is possible danger.

You put on your fear spectacles, where all you see is potential danger.

SUMMARY OF FLIGHT OR FIGHT

The fight-or-flight response will be triggered if you feel threatened; your body's survival system will be activated releasing adrenaline that promotes a survival reaction within you perceiving everything in your situation as a possible threat to your survival. You observe everything in your world as a potential threat to your survival. Your fear is magnified and you will not be thinking clearly. You will see everything as dangerous and potentially harmful. Your view of the world is one of fear.

EFFECT OF THE MOON ON YOUR EMOTIONS

When you acquire a deeper understanding of how the moon can affect you mentally and emotionally you will be able to apply the tools and techniques to aid your own healing and you will have more control over your own health.

If the phases of the moon are not relevant in everyday life then why do diaries indicate the dates of the full moon? The reason being is that the moon plays a large roll on our emotional state, in particular a full moon. Most people definitely experience a specific change in their emotions and behaviour, however they are unaware of what is making them feel this way. The effect of the full moon is greater in females as opposed to males because females display different emotions due to the moon being of female energy. Men will definitely feel the effects although maybe not as strong as the female species.

The moon is female energy and is said to rule over women and the twenty eight/twenty nine day cycle to it becoming full is a similar amount of time as the female's menstrual cycle. If you think about fishermen, they work with the moon and its gravitational force that causes the sea tides to ebb and flow.

The moon is a powerful force that coordinates the tides. It is no different with the female menstruation cycle as our bodies are 90% water; this is why we feel emotional or weepy during the times of our periods. It could be that the moon disturbs the association of water molecules in the nervous system.

You must know people who seem really nice and then wham bam once a month they change and become quite emotional, intensely stressed, and lose focus or concentration. Try watching for these moods swings and check your diary and make a note of the date and twenty eight/nine days later they are off again. The cycle is endless. The effects of the full moon are generally 4 to 5 days before it is at its fullest and two or three days after it is at its fullest, although it all depends on you.

Research performed at Leeds University showed that the general practitioners consultations are increased by around 3% during a full moon.

Not everyone is affected by the full moon. If you feel that you are one of the lucky people who are unaffected by the full moon then by looking at it from a different perspective the full moon can be a time of clarification for you to expel outdated influences in your life. The full moon energy can be very positive for you to concentrate on your true desires. The full moon is also a positive time making plans and for discharging negative patterns.

I do not profess to be an expert about the moon it is all down to me being consciously aware of how I am feeling and keeping an eye out the week prior to the full moon.

I personally buy a moon calendar every year it is so beneficial having it hanging on the wall. If you learn to understand the moon phases you are in a better position to understand your reactions and moods and therefore deal with these in a more assertive and positive way.

EXERCISE

Firstly check the date of the next full moon

Take a pad and write down anything that you would like to release and let go both physically and emotionally. eg a bad relationship or a lack of money

Make sure to set your intention and focus on releasing what you have written down, before and during the exercise.

Once you have released everything go outside, set the piece of paper alight and burn it.

Now just release all attachment and wait for the magic to unfold.

SPECIAL NOTE

If you have suffered and are recovering from a traumatic event, remember that it takes time to heal, everyone is unique and therefore heals in their own way and time.

If quite a time has passed and your symptoms are not getting any better, then please seek professional help.

CHAPTER THREE
EMOTIONAL GUIDANCE

Are you aware to what degree do your emotions control your everyday life?

There are two basic emotions that have such an intense impact on your life and they are love and fear. I mention love first because love is the foundation of everything. We all have the golden thread of love running through us, it is just discovering it, and once you do discover it, it will be a bobbin of endless golden thread of unconditional love.

A beautiful affirmation to repeat as much as possible is:

> **I am enriched with unconditional love, in my mind, body and spirit**
> -Grace Brown

LOVE AND FEAR

Love and fear cannot be present together. Once you understand this and you are consciously aware of this, you will have greater control over your life. Where there is love, fear cannot be present. Where there is fear, love will not be present. Whichever becomes most prominent the other will depart!

Let us say that you are having a picnic and having a really good time with plenty of fun and laughter. Your mobile phone rings and someone explains that an important person close to you has suddenly taken ill, you rapidly feel sick at the pit of your stomach and very scared, the love has disappeared, replaced by the fear, it has gone!

The fears that are very deep within us are really things that have been ingrained within us by our conditioning, our belief system from being very young. A friend of my mum's had such fear about cats; she would break out in hot sweats at the thought of a cat.

Automatically my friend has grown up with a fear of cats, and she now has two little boys who, yes you have guessed it are scared to death of cats. The fears do not really exist, we simply believe they do, so we are held captive imprisoned by our emotional fears.

Fear can be overcome by love though, love conquers everything. Universal Gardens' releasing and letting go will assist you in conquering fear. If you are suddenly afraid of something you can dig deep and discover the end of the golden thread of love and you will feel immediately better.

You have a choice as to whether to choose love or fear. Everything in life is down to choice, choose wisely, and choose love.

> Never be afraid to try something new.
> Remember, amateurs built the ark,
> professionals built the Titanic.
>
> Author Unknown

LOVE AND FEAR BASED WORDS

Are you aware that 7% of your communication is words only? 93% of communication is non-verbal.

Each word just like a thought carries a vibration and words are powerful, whether positive or negative. Your thoughts are constructed by words and words draw circumstances and events to you. Many circumstances of which you do not desire. You are probably not aware of your own personal verbal communication and the powerful effect it has on you and on others too. The words that you use give a good indication as to where your thoughts are centred. Sometimes when we speak we are not consciously aware of the negative words we are using because they are so ingrained within us.

Negative wording was brought to my attention by a tutor of mine many years ago. I went through a very dark time about 7 years ago and times were very tough, I was forever saying I don't want to be poor or I don't want to be always paying my bills late or I don't want to worry all of the time and many more negative connotations. I was definitely negative about many things and that was echoed through my wording.

The universe cannot distinguish between certain words like

NO

NOT

CAN'T

Therefore when I was saying

"I don't want to be poor"
the universe would read it as

"I want to be poor".

"I don't want to be always paying my bills late"
would be read as

"I want to be always paying my bills late"

" I don't want to worry all of the time"
would suggest

"I want to worry all of the time".

So eliminate the words

WANT, DON'T NO, NOT, CAN'T

, WANT NEVER GETS

If you say "I want to be rich" the universe will interpret that you want to be rich and keep you wanting, so exchange want to "desire".

You only have one chance to make a first impression, and it is on that first impression that people shape their feelings about you. If your words are negative and your life is not as you would desire all you need to do is modify your thought processing and wording.

You gain strength, courage, and confidence
by every experience in which you really stop
to look fear in the face...
The danger lies in refusing to face the fear,
in not daring to come to grips with it...
You must make yourself succeed every time.
You must do the thing you think you cannot do.

Eleanor Roosevelt

Below is a table of love and fear based words, have a look at them and see which words strike a chord with you.

If you use the word unhappy frequently exchange it for gratitude and make gratitude your way of life.

Love Based Thoughts	Fear Based Thoughts
Gratitude	Unhappiness
Joy	Sadness
Trust	Apprehension
Satisfaction	Controlling
Kindness	Inconsideration
Consideration	Coldness
Compassion	Abhorrence
Integrity	Dishonesty
Pleasure	Afraid
Delight	Frightened
Happiness	Paranoia
Enlightenment	Intimidation
Determined	Alarming
Positivity	Pessimism
Enthral	Terror
Affectionate	Dread

BLOCKING OUT EMOTIONS

The most important thing that you never do with emotions is to block them out. People who block their emotions are likely to suffer serious mental, emotional and physical illness. Suppressed and repressed emotions have a way of sneaking back up to the surface at some point. If not processed, they come out in inappropriate ways; as opposed to those who face up to their emotions, feeling and accepting them, resulting in the emotions being processed and worked through to a positive outcome.

EXERCISE

When emotions are processed and felt they diminish,
ease and release all together.

To prevent these emotions and feelings building up,
spend time each day in one of 'The Universal Gardens'
connecting with your mind, body and spirit.

When your emotions are triggered,
give yourself time and space to feel it and allow it to be processed.

If you can do this daily it will help to prevent a buildup.

**Fear defeats more people
than any other one thing in the world.**
Ralph Waldo Emerson

EMOTIONAL GUIDANCE POINTERS

It is your emotions that affect the way you think, feel, act and react

※

Good emotions are indicators of you being on the right track

※

Emotions have a huge influence on your physical body

※

If you repress emotions, it is highly likely that illnesses will occur

※

Emotions that are not processed and released will be
hidden deep within the body or within your energy field, the aura

When certain emotions are not processed they are the source of
very serious illnesses, including cancer, emotional illness of the mind,
arthritis and many other types of chronic illnesses

※

Negative emotions such as fear, anxiety, negativity, frustration and
depression cause chemical reactions in your body that are very different
from the chemicals released when you feel positive emotions
such as happy, content, loved and accepted

> We are all tattooed in our cradles
> with the beliefs of our tribe;
> the record may seem superficial, but it is indelible.

> You cannot educate a man wholly out of the
> superstitious fears which were implanted
> in his imagination,
> no matter how utterly his reason may reject them.
>
> Oliver Wendell Holmes

Chapter Four
Belief Systems

Nature has so built man that he has absolute control over the material which reaches the subconscious mind, through his five senses, although this is not meant to be construed as a statement that man always exercises this control.

Napoleon Hill

Our beliefs are thought patterns that we have developed since infancy, some of which serve us well, however, the majority of them do not. We all have our own personal belief system that governs our thoughts, words, and deeds. Thoughts and beliefs are essential as our belief system is essentially our makeup and makes up who we are and what we are.

What we believe or perceive to be true creates our thoughts and in turn creates our reality, which in some cases can restrict the life we are leading if we are thinking negatively. All beliefs, thoughts and ideas that your mind is conditioned to have become a part of you and therefore that is who you become. Our beliefs define our lives and allow exceptional things for those who understand the importance of our beliefs.

Always remember that you always attract into your life what you focus on and believe to be true. So if you believe you cannot afford to make ends meet, then you will not. Look closely at the people in your life, are they optimistic and are you optimistic? Are they happy and are you happy? Do they seem to be reacting to the same circumstances time and time again and are you? After studying this you will see that you and the people in your life are experiencing the same situations and circumstances time and time again. Believe me it is like a self fulfilling prophecy.

The time it will take to establish new beliefs into your mind will depend upon how you process your new thought patterns. Most people spend their time thinking about what has happened in the past good or bad; these thoughts influence what will occur in the future good or bad.

If you plant a seed in the ground, you will take great care in choosing the seed, you will water it, nurture it and weed the garden to eliminate the weeds, your mind is no different as beliefs are really nothing more than thoughts (seeds) or our ideas that we believe to be true; it is literally your belief in your thoughts that is what makes them so dominating and powerful.

Try to plant your thoughts (seeds) with awareness because in effect you are planting seeds on purpose for the dreams and desires for your future. If the weeds (negative thoughts) establish their roots in the garden of your mind you will find that you will be overrun by these toxic negative weeds (thoughts) and they will eventually take up permanent roots again and destroy your future dreams and desires.

We are free to think and believe whatever we desire; however once you flip the switch to change your beliefs, you are literally changing your reality. If your life is not how you would like it to be you simply flip the switch to change your beliefs.

Our belief system is formed from being very young and we accept our beliefs as our definitive truth and find it very difficult not to believe in them. In order of making a change in your life, it is essential to modify your belief system and identify your standards by believing that you are worthy and deserve prosperity in your life now.

What the mind can conceive and believe, the mind can achieve

Napoleon Hill

Begin to nurture your garden and its positive seeds by consciously choosing wisely about what you would wish to produce. REMEMBER that the positive seeds have to have constant attention and care paid to them. If you wish to have different outcomes in your life, then you must provide your mind with new directions to pursue. Your prevailing thoughts decide upon what your reality will be.

So we have now established that our beliefs are the foundation of what we experience which is fantastic, however what is the next step?

> If your life is not as you would wish it to be,
> things are not too great for you or
> maybe prosperity is eluding you, fear not,
> you have not missed the boat
> it is never too late to start again.
> Believing is achieving.
>
> Grace Brown

Key Point...

Firstly pay attention to your negative thoughts which are the weeds.

See the thought for what it is, it is merely a negative thought (weed) that can be changed because you are the one in control.

So pull out that weed, they are your thoughts and your thoughts alone!

People are confined by their thoughts.

One of my tutors showed me a great thing for weeding my garden; she explained that if I placed an elastic band or silicone band on my wrist, each time that I had a negative thought I was to move it to the other hand and turn the negative thought into a positive one. Oh my word it began to work, after a while my wrists were so sore with swapping it all of the time I simply didn't have many bad thoughts left, it did the trick.

Another thing that you can do is to have a piece of raw amethyst (around about two inches long) on your desk at work, each time that a negative thought comes in to your head move the stone to the other side of the desk, you can even keep it in your pocket and just keep swapping them around.

HOW TO CHANNEL THE AMAZING POWER OF YOUR THOUGHTS...

Always be aware that energy follows thought.
However a thought is just a thought and a thought can be changed

It is important that you realise that by focusing on something,
you energise that thought and therefore
that thought will eventually become reality

If you are constantly thinking the same thoughts this means
that the thoughts will be highly energised and have
more control over your reality, so if you think that you have
lack in your life, then lack will prevail

Our beliefs are powerful and we can only create our lives
by our belief and what we believe to be true

Let go of the negatives and take control of the positive things in
your life and listen to your thoughts, the more you increase your
consciousness of your belief system, the more that you can
restructure it to create the life that you desire

Change how you view things.
When you do you will begin to experience changes within.
You will begin to experience life in a completely different way

Believing is a powerful thing, just as the word belief is a strong,
powerful and meaningful word and therefore also creative.
Believing is yang, strong, positive, energetic and
very much active and functioning

Not believing is firstly dull, unhealthy, unconstructive,
lifeless, uncreative and negative

From your beliefs your reality is formed
Grace Brown

Chapter Five
The Layers of an Onion

If we looked at our lives as layers, like the layers of an onion and like the onion there are so many layers to each of us, when we peel back the first layer it then reveals another layer and another and so forth.

This is exactly like our lives, like the onion our layers have to be peeled back in order of identifying the real you. The onion outer skin is relatively easy to peel back, however when we move past a few layers and get nearer to the core, the rings seem to be tightly compacted. The tightly compacted substance close to the core has been there a very long time, bubbling away all these years.

The layers of life include sadness, pain, hurt, relationship breakdowns and a great deal more that is entwined around the core of their hearts. Sadly, it is also the sadness, pain, anger and the not forgiving yourself or others that is entwined around your heart. These feeling and emotions that are in our heart centre or our core have been stuck there for a long time, bubbling away for many years.

Within each and every one of us there is a storehouse within your subconscious mind of your beliefs. Many people live in the past (many with memories of some suffering or sadness) and therefore allow their past to create their future because they are not living in the present.

You will find that if you peel back the onion whether it makes you cry or not, it will be very good for you. By peeling back the layers we are able to move on in life and go forwards as opposed to backwards, changing gradually and at a gentle pace.

Some things are lodged so deep within us, hiding inside; we have buried them so deep within us not allowing these feelings to come out. We have learned to disguise our feelings from our family, friends and loved ones. In some cases by holding back these emotions it can have detrimental effects on our relationships. It all depends upon how stuck or obstructed the emotional energy is; releasing these emotions is not going to be easy as it means facing up to your your fears and demons.

I like to consider myself a happy onion because I understand my emotions and know my true inner essence. My onion centre is one of immense belief, faith and connection to source energy, the universe and my beautiful angels and for that I am a really happy grateful onion, woo hoo!

So, if you would like to become a happy onion then you have to take responsibility for yourself by taking great care of your emotions and feelings at the very core of your being, just like the centre of the onion.

Taking care of your emotions is the greatest gift that you can give to yourself. We have to be in tune with our core which is our onion centre and take good care of our health and wellbeing. To do this you have to continually clear away any unwanted debris keeping ourselves in emotionally tip top condition.

Chapter Six
Intentions

Intentions are set moment-to-moment

We have all set an intention or intentions in the past that most of us are unable to connect with the power behind this intention. On a daily basis we are forever creating our intentions. When we consciously create we will dramatically change the life that we are living, making it possible for us to take steps to attracting the life of our dreams.

You will discover as we move through this section that intentions that are set consciously are the things that will bring to you, your desires and dreams. Therefore, it is imperative that you place your full ATTENTION, in other words your focus, on your INTENTION. When you are consciously aware of your intentions you are in fact a powerful manifester, you have the power to create the things that you desire in all areas of your life.

Did you know that intentions are energy?

> **It is not the words that make a difference it is the intention that fuels the words!**
>
> Grace Brown

If you have an idea about something this is a thought, now, an intention is different because it is a choice, a choice that is made by you; it is a decision as intentions are energy. Thought is energy in motion, so when we think of our intention we are in fact sending a vibrational message to the universe regarding what we desire to manifest. With each intention we activate our creative flow. Creative flow is good; it simply means that we are creating our experiences in life consciously, or on purpose. It is very important that we fully understand that our conscious intentions will create the life of our dreams and sadly the unconscious intentions are the ones that will create chaos in our life, this is because we are not focusing our intent.

I really cannot emphasise enough that your energy goes where your attention flows. When you are focusing your attention, you are paying attention, holding your attention, the Buddhist monks call it mindfulness, holding your attention on something is crucial to how your life turns out. It is important to realise that you are aware that intentions, and your ability to consciously or unconsciously create them, is the most powerful amazing creative tool that you possess.

STRONG AND WEAK INTENTIONS

Depending upon the length of time given to each desire some intentions will be fragile, whilst others will be powerful and strong. The problem being is that, we follow our thoughts, usually one thought after another and another, the majority of these thoughts are negative.

The fragile or weak intentions will not manifest or come into fruition due to them being weak, however the strong intentions will although they may take a longer time to manifest.

This is not because they are more difficult to bring into fruition it is down to how long you can actually embrace the feeling...everything is about feeling...feeling your way to what you desire, as if it is already happening in the here and now (acting as if)!

The longer that you can hold onto an intention with an excited reaction, is relative to how long it will take to become apparent in your reality.

SETTING INTENTIONS

When I decide to set my intention on something I know that it is right for me, and I feel good. Your gut instinct will always let you know that your intentions are the correct ones. Look at intentions as having and acting with purpose. Look to seize every opportunity and walk through every door that is open to you.

Every day my intention is to be, do and be the finest that I can be, offering kindness and love and a smile to the people I meet on my journey of life. Every day I live in the present moment, the now, as I am so aware that the now creates my future and each day I live it as if it is my last day as I am a co-creator of my reality.

How to use the Power of Intention...

Set your intention to be the best and have the finest desires.

Set your intention on love and kindness and smile a lot.

Always be in the present moment.

Know that you are a creator of your reality.

> Quality is never an accident;
> it is always the result of high intention,
> sincere effort, intelligent direction
> and skilful execution. . . .
>
> Willa A. Foster

Choosing Intentions

Whichever Universal Garden you decide to go into will work with you to set specific intentions. It is important to have vision and set your intention by choosing your intention and specify it in writing in your journal. When you set your intention try to be as specific as you possibly can be. You see when you set your intention and take steps to demonstrate your commitment; it is like watching the magic happen as wonderful things come about.

You have to believe in yourself and have blind faith that you can achieve your intention. Your intentions will help you in taking better control of your life. Believe in your ability to place your attention on your INTENTION. Creating a practical action plan that will get you from where you are in your life now to where you desire to be is essential.

Our intentions that we plan to create, have to be powerful. If our intentions are not powerful, we are in fact not really having creative intentions; we therefore are reducing our creative power. We are giving away our creative power to another. Be aware of what you are giving away, take stock and take charge.

So let us break it down into baby steps...

The first step - decide what your intention is and what you need to do

Decide what and if any changes you would like to make in your life or changes about you. It maybe that you decide to change your home, where you live, a new hair colour, create financial freedom, body shape, weight loss-gain or in fact anything that you desire to change at all

Look at your belief system and see if any of your beliefs or your outlook needs to be changed. Our viewpoint or our outlook on our lives has a huge impact on the way we live our lives, the way we approach our confrontations and even on the length of our life

Use your gut instinct by feeling your way, learn to feel, feel that it is the right intention. Feel...feel with feeling... and feel...feel...feel...your way through life

Try to see your intention as a goal and act as if your goal is already achieved. Visualise your intention in action, as though you can see yourself with your desire in action and with movement, feel it and feel the emotion of achieving your desire, of you having it now and how good it feels

Appreciate and remember that you can eat an elephant if you so desire, however you can only eat the elephant one bite at a time

Change your pessimistic viewpoint if you have one (unknowingly as time has gone by you may have developed a negative attitude on life) to a more optimistic one.
Your viewpoint or outlook on how you perceive life to be can have a massive impact on the way that you live your life, also in the way that you face your challenges or obstacles (see them as your stepping stones to success)

Make it your intention to release any feelings of resentment and work through a forgiveness process for yourself.

A great affirmation for intentions is "I offer my intentions of love and joy to my subconscious mind, for them to come into fruition now"

.... I am convinced that life is 10% what happens to me and 90% how I react to it."

Charles Swindoll

Key Point...

Have unwavering faith.

When we decide to set an intention we have to be one hundred percent unwavering on achieving our intention in the near future.

So therefore it is important that you are grounded in the present moment as your intention will require your focus, attention, control, power and clarity to assist you in bringing your intention into fruition.

There can be no distractions, you have to be totally dedicated in bringing it into your own reality.

It is important that you are aware that your intentions help you to take control of your life.

The remarkable thing is we have a choice every day regarding the attitude we will embrace for that day.

We cannot change our past . . . we cannot change the fact that people will act in a certain way. We cannot change the inevitable.

The only thing we can do is play on the one string we have, and that is our attitude.

Keep your dreams alive.
Understand to achieve anything
requires faith and belief in yourself, vision, hard
work, determination, and dedication.

Remember all things are possible
for those who believe.
Gail Devers

CHAPTER SEVEN
FORGIVENESS

> When you are angry,
> it is as if you a holding a burning coal.
> Your anger is affecting only you and until you release
> it, you will continue to do so.
>
> Buddha

In life, in order to move on in this life you have to make a decision to forgive, as forgiving means that you are living in the present moment as opposed to the past.

It does not mean that you can forget everything; however it does mean that you can release obstacles and learn to move on.

Forgiveness means you are letting go of your anger against who or whatever has hurt you and in the process releasing the weight of the past hurt, pain and anger you feel.

You can finally begin to heal.

> The magic happens
> when we learn to cast out the burdens
> and forgive ourselves and others.
>
> Grace Brown

I know that when you refuse to offer forgiveness you are the only victim. The person that has hurt you will not feel the emotions you are feeling, they will not be aware of how you feel. You always have a choice in being the forgiver or of being the victim! Which are you?

Constantly reliving your feeling of hurt gives the individual who caused your upset power over you. Have you heard the old saying 'it sticks like glue'? This is exactly what happens when you cling on to hurt, feelings of resentment, bitterness and in some cases deep emotional hatred.

So many areas of your life can suffer, in particularly your health. By holding onto these emotions and the urge to have revenge, can harm you, when you hold on to them for long periods of time they then build up and become lodged in your body as stuck energy.

> **Not forgiving someone is like drinking poison and expecting the other person to die.**
> Carrie Fisher

Your defensive thoughts will be running through your head constantly, like a dark cloud, hovering over you. You will feel as though there is a huge dark cloud of negative energy hanging over you and thoughts of revenge will be going around your mind in a never-ending cycle.

I have had so many angry people state that the best form of defence is attack. This is an automatic response to attack whilst being defensive; however this is not the correct approach; FORGIVENESS is the key to moving on in life.

Key Point...

By not forgiving someone, you may feel that you are getting one over on them or causing them pain, this is not the case because the only person that you are hurting is yourself.

You are probably thinking I cannot forgive, I will never forgive or I do not wish to forgive.......

You can, I know you can because I did.

Having a very rigid viewpoint means that you cannot move on without forgiving.

What you believe to be true in your mind ultimately affects the quality of your well being, attitude, and your relationships.

Forgiveness offers a mental cleansing, releasing the poison within.

Grace Brown

For example, before going to sleep

write in your journal who or what you wish to forgive.
When we sleep we are still creating and it is in the dream state
that the subconscious mind will offer you solutions
to current blockages in your life.

By writing in your journal before you go to sleep
you will be planting the seeds of forgiveness,
nurturing solutions to your problems

A PERSONAL EXPERIENCE OF JULIE

In 2006 I began offering workshops to help people to move on in their lives and on my first workshop I met Julie. Julie came along with a friend, she was lovely, quiet and shy, however above all I detected that she had personal emotional issues. One of the first subjects we touched on was forgiveness.

Out of the twenty five people she was the only person not to have any input during the conversing of forgiveness, however during refreshments she came and chatted to me. During the conversation she explained that her husband had left her with three children aged between fifteen to twenty and that she could never forgive him, I smiled and said you will and quite firmly she replied I will not.

When it came to lunch Julie sat next to me and explained that her elder son was getting married and she would like to have made him a collage of photographs from being young to his present age. Julie went on to explain that she could not because Julie's ex husband had all of the photographs.

I asked her to have faith and trust in the Universe to deliver her photographs, however firstly to release the obstacles she must try to offer forgiveness to her husband and to herself also, to which she replied I will try but I do not hold out much faith.

I said to Julie firstly forgive and then have faith in your heart and wait for the magic to happen.

From that workshop ten people asked if I would start a local group of which I did and Julie was one of them. So, the group commenced the following month on the Tuesday evening and Julie came in all smiles and gave me a big hug and enlightened me with her news that she had been trying to forgive every day and was feeling a little better about everything.

The next meeting she came in gushing with great news she had been clearing out some cupboards and in between some stuff a little parcel fell out and guess what it was, yes it was a duplicate set of photos of the children, which meant that she could now make her photograph collage for her son's wedding.

Forgiveness is an action of the mind. It challenges you to enjoy being here in the NOW and envisage an enhanced future.

It challenges you to face up to releasing your negative thoughts about the circumstances and to have faith in believing that you have an improved future.

It brings together self-belief proving that you can survive the pain and grow and learn from it.

"Forgiveness is the golden key to discover the golden thread of love that runs through you"

Grace Brown

Unless you have the energy of forgiveness, there will be no room for any changes to take place.

The power to mentally free yourself is within you, you have the power to free yourself from the negativity of being unforgiving; the power is within you.

I believe that the Universe sees the workings of our hearts and forgiveness is working from the heart. Universally our good intentions will be recognised from our forgiveness.

Intention is the most important thing that matters.

The weak can never forgive. Forgiveness is an attribute of the strong
Mahatma Gandhi

Exercise to Forgive 1

If you have been hurt by someone the best way to deal with the hurt you are feeling is to firstly understand why you are feeling so hurt. If someone has hurt you that you love, for the love and respect to continue you have to discover ways of bringing closure to the situation that is acceptable to all concerned.

As human beings we should all have respect for each other and just because you love someone does not mean that you have to like how they behave.

Offering forgiveness does not mean that you are giving permission for their actions and behaviour.
Forgiveness in your heart is what is required;
forgiveness is a course of action for the healing to take place.

The easiest way to deal with a situation is to write a letter to the offender (this is a hugely powerful way to focus your attention). Setting aside a little time to write it down will help you to process your emotions, see the problem in a different light and work your way towards a solution.

Recognise what is positive in the relationship and express forgiveness for the negative part of the relationship that hurts you.
It is of great importance that you allow yourself to express all your feelings fully.

Do not post it or allow the offender see it, this is not a letter to the offender but to the Universe.
To post your letter to the Universe we do not need a stamp.

Take the letter outside and burn it thereby sending it out it into the Universe for the healing to begin to take place.

Exercise to Forgive 2

You will require:
- A clean piece of paper or a pad, and a pen.
- A white tea light candle (unscented).
- A piece of white alabaster gemstone.

(The white alabaster is known as a "drawing" stone. It has the ability to draw things to you or to repel things away from you)

Or use a piece of pink calcite as this is a stone of support and encourages forgiveness.

Before commencing to write your letter of forgiveness:

Move yourself into a comfortable position (I personally sit upright in a high backed chair with my feet firmly on the ground).

Adjust your body until you feel comfortable. Place you hands (palms facing upwards) on your thighs and relax.

Now, spend several minutes merely observing your natural breathing as you are breathing in and out rhythmically, feel the chest and abdomen rise and fall, notice how the air passes through your nostrils and throat or if you are breathing through your mouth the sensation of exhaling through your lips. Now notice that without any effort on your part at all your breathing has slowed down of its own accord.

Now, you will need to take a very slow and controlled deep breath counting 1-2-3-4 and hold for 1-2-3-4 and release for 1-2-3-4, repeat this three times.

Now, slowly breathe in on a count of 1-2-3-4-5-6 (either through the nose or through the mouth, the nose is better if you can), and hold your breath for the count of 1-2-3-4-5-6, exhale slowly for a count of 1-2-3-4-5-6, repeat three times.

This will help to keep your breathing steady and even.

EXERCISE TO FORGIVE 2 (CONTINUED)

This particular breathing technique will also give your body an oxygen blast that will enable you to relax further.

More than likely thoughts and images may come into your mind, simply allow them to come in and to go straight out paying them no attention at all. You are now relaxed and focused and ready to begin writing down your thoughts of forgiveness.

This cleansing process will bring about a calm, quiet awareness, how fantastic is that!

Next you need to actually write down that you forgive yourself or the person responsible for this act and that you are releasing your anger and hurt.

Make a list of what and who you wish to forgive, what was actually done that caused your pain and forgive and let go.

Next, write down that you are now going to move on in your life and that you wish them well in theirs. We should never wish negative things on anyone as the law of attraction returns your thoughts, words and deeds back to you like a boomerang, so wish the person well.

Finally, at the end of the letter write this affirmation:

"I release all negativity from my mind, body and aura"

This is an amazing affirmation that I have used over the years, particularly with forgiveness, it simply makes you feel as though you are casting your burdens out. I used this particular affirmation probably fifty times a day when I was in the process of forgiving someone very close to me (a family member) and believe me it worked.

Writing things down actually bring them to the forefront of your awareness and helps you to see them from a completely different viewpoint giving you clarity, and having clarity makes it so much easier.

Now, this brings you to the hardest part.... forgetting. You will always have the scar; however, you will not bring the injury to the surface again. You have not erased the memory of the act; however, to forget can only be achieved by the act of true forgiveness. In the fullness of time you will realise that to forget is to forgive.

> The forgiving acquires honours here
> and a state of blessedness hereafter.
> Those men that ever conquer their wrath
> by forgiveness obtain the higher regions.
> Therefore has it been said that
> forgiveness is the highest virtue.
> The Mahabharata

Reconciliation

The question that most people ask me is if I can forgive can I reconcile the relationship? My response to that is reconciliation is a process that moves far beyond forgiveness. Once you realise that something is broken, our natural instinct is to attempt to repair it. However the work of reconciliation is not an easy task. Reconciliation means that two people have to come to an agreement, it is all about trying to achieve some light from the darkness.

Reconciliation maybe achieved if the person that has been hurt has forgiven the person responsible, or together they have agreed a positive outcome to their relationship. However this rarely happens as this generally requires an experienced third party who can liaise with everyone that is implicated in the conflict.

If you do not endeavour to see that there are two sides to everything, then the problem that you have will never begin to heal. If the person has said that they are sorry, and have promised to avoid any further situations like this one, surely everyone deserves a second chance.

> Friends, partners and family are what keep us on our toes and make us happy. Don't let it go because of a weak moment.

Six Tips to Reconciliation

In order of bridging the gap between you and the perpetrator
you will have to release any anger and negative emotions,
otherwise reconciliation simply will not happen

It is important that you do not focus on the past events
by asking questions about the circumstances leading up to the episode.
You see what is done is done; you cannot change the past
however you can change how you view it

It is so important that you live in the present moment
and ensure that you are all in agreement to not allow
the episode to come to the surface again,
make the most of what you have now
and be grateful that you have been able to salvage the relationship

All parties need to take responsibility for the situation;
it is best that the offender is not asked to defend or
justify their part or actions in the situation.
It is simply best to let go as letting go is the definitive answer

The pain and hurt will diffuse considerably once you begin
to look outwards and see the big picture
rather than looking inwards and seeing a tiny pin hole

You do not have to reconcile the relationship in order to forgive

If you find that certain doors are closed to you this is a signal that the direction in which you are heading is not in your best interests, trust!

Grace Brown

RECONCILIATION OF TWO VERY DEAR FRIENDS WHO FORGAVE

Janice and Sue had been the dearest of friends for around fifteen years. But, Janice basically controlled Sue's every move. Sue managed to secure a permanent position within a local company. Very quickly she worked her way up through the ranks to a very good position in the company.

With her new found responsibility she was working longer hours and working away from home more and more and began not intentionally to move away from Janice. However, Janice was not happy with her friend for not being there as she had previously been and the relationship was becoming more and more difficult due to Janice's unreasonable demands and jealousy.

Although Sue's life was becoming pretty complete at work she was still missing one thing a loving relationship with a partner. Well this was all about to change, she met a nice chap Toby and embarked on the journey of love; her life was literally becoming complete.

Janice's jealousy went through the roof at not only the career success of Sue but now she had romantic fulfilment. Sue and Toby's relationship blossomed so much and so quickly that they bought a house together and moved in, madly in love and very happy.

This became too much for Janice to control her jealousy. At Sue's and Toby's house warming jealousy got the better of Janice. Fuelled by alcohol and jealousy Janice made an obvious and over the top attempt to seduce Toby in front of everyone including Sue.

Not only did Janice lose her dignity that night, she lost the friendship of everyone at the party especially Sue. Sue completely disowned Janice refusing to take her calls the friendship was over in her eyes.

Three years past and Sue found out one day through a friend that Janice had been diagnosed with Breast Cancer and that her long term survival was very slim. Sue thought about the last three years without Janice in her life and realised there was a void, and if Janice died there would be an even bigger void and therefore made the decision to forgive her.

Sue contacted Janice and they met up and through a lot of hugs and tears made up their differences, Janice was so apologetic of her terrible jealousy and Sue forgave her.

During the last 18months of Janice's life the two women became even closer than they were before. During Janice's final days Sue looked after Janice like she was an only sister and was with her when she died.

Sue was so glad that she had been given the opportunity to say goodbye to Janice, this opportunity was given to Sue through her being able to simply forgive.

Forgive and watch how your life transforms, just like magic.

HOW TO CHANGE YOUR LIFE WITH FORGIVENESS...

Forgive when you feel ready, however sooner is better than later

Always remember that you can begin the forgiveness process whenever you feel ready

Forgiveness cannot be forced, it has to happen when you are ready and not before

Forgiveness gives you freedom

See forgiveness as a gift that you give to yourself.

Grace Brown

CHAPTER EIGHT
AFFIRMATIONS

Did you know that you can change your mind with the help of affirmations?

Affirmations and auto suggestion (auto-suggestion is basically self-suggestion) are a very important tool to change and enhance your personal development.

Affirmations are simply positive statements that are either read out loud or written down, and when this is done time and time again will begin to change the way the sub conscious mind feels and more importantly assumes this is the case.

Affirmations to me are the foundations of self-improvement. They have helped me greatly to transform my life and totally enhanced my sense of worth. I promise you that if you follow all of the tips and advice in this section and continue several times a day you will achieve the benefit.

Affirmations have not only the capacity to create changes in situations and circumstances; they also help to eradicate negative thinking providing that you are working with the correct affirmations for your circumstances and on a regular basis.

Affirmations must always be fuelled with positive energy and in the present tense; it is this good energy that extends outward to create change. It is important that you always try to see the end result or the final outcome of whatever you desire to change in your life. More importantly have blind faith in your affirmations taking form because affirmations are all about believing and trusting in them coming into fruition.

Do not allow doubt to creep in, because if you do, your desire will not happen. By not believing or taking the affirmation rituals seriously you are not showing faith. Always have faith and know that your desire will manifest in your reality and be patient.

If you do have a problem in remembering to recite, or write your affirmations, you can always affirm that you perform your affirmations daily "I am grateful that I recite my affirmations daily"!

There are certain ways of phrasing Affirmations in order to make them effective.
When we work with affirmations either spoken or written, their impact may be stronger on some more than others.

It all depends upon the individual. Some people find it very difficult to slow the mind down because their minds are constantly whizzing around with the everyday things in life.

The purpose here is to help you to bring order to your chaotic mind so that it enables you to have some serenity whilst reciting your affirmations.

You have power within you

Take charge of this power and create the life of your dreams, remember the journey of a thousand miles began with the first step, take that first step today and always remember when creating anything it has to be for your highest good and the highest good of others. There is magic in every one's mind; let us together bring out the magic in your mind.

I have an amazing recipe for a carrot cake. Before I decide to bake my cake I have a check list of what ingredients are required and what weight everything has to be. When making up your affirmations it is no different to baking a cake really, it is all about the ingredients (the content) and the emotion and the belief that your (affirmations) cake will turn out perfectly.

How to Use the Power of Affirmations...

The affirmation must always be in the present tense.

Firstly write down the affirmation.
(My partner uses an affirmation journal as he finds this more disciplined and effective).
Now, read the affirmation back to yourself several times; once you are familiar with the sentence recite the affirmation out verbally whilst visualising your desire or desired outcome.
E.g. If you desire financial freedom your affirmation would be
"I am so grateful for my financial freedom, thank you"
As you recite the affirmation imagine how it would feel to have financial freedom now.

Always remain focussed when either writing or reciting your daily affirmations.

Believe in the power of your affirmations, have unrelenting faith.

Declare the affirmation in a clear, firm voice with a great big cheesy grin on your face as you say them.

Affirmations can be very powerful for anything you desire to achieve.

Affirmations must always be positive as they can establish your life and give additional energy to your life; this additional positive energy will boost the creativity of your desired reality; on the other hand if the additional energy is based on, worry, lack, fear or anything negative then you will receive those things.

Affirmations should not consist of negative wording (don't, cannot etc) only use positive affirming words in the present tense.

Dream as if you'll live forever,
live as if you'll die today.

James Dean

During my seminars and training days so many people tell me that they struggle to remember to do their affirmations or they do not have time to do their affirmations.

Of course you have time, you must treat your affirmations like you would any other daily duty. Do you forget to clean your teeth each day, feed the dog or pick the kids up from school each day?

Of course not! Treat your affirmations as a daily necessity, by doing this you will not forget to do your affirmations. Get into the habit of reciting your affirmations while doing mundane daily tasks like cleaning your teeth, showering, cleaning, hoovering or driving. You see we all spend hours a day doing mundane tasks so really we all have plenty of time to recite our affirmations daily.

Using affirmations on a daily basis you will boost your positive energy and attract what you predominantly desire into your world.

> **A mind troubled by doubt cannot focus on the course to victory.**
> Arthur Golden

MY PERSONAL EXPERIENCE WITH AFFIRMATIONS

I am going to share with you a very personal experience that I really do not like to think about because it is in the past and therefore should stay there, however I truly believe that you will understand from this experience that no matter where you are in your life, you have the power and capabilities to do something positive and change your life for the better.

It is very difficult to be bouncing off the walls with positivity when you feel like your world is crumbling around you, I know because I have been in dire financial situations and in fact lost everything, my home, business, dignity, self worth and the saddest things of all friends; friends that I adored who were successful and wealthy in their own rights. However, they saw me as a failure and completely dropped me like a stone, perhaps not as true friends as I thought; of course I have forgiven them.

When it all happened I could not face anyone, I was so afraid of answering the door in case it was another bailiff and literally showered in a morning and took my sleeping pills and anti depressants and stayed in bed until the next morning, I was leading a nonexistent life, I simply could not cope, I was so scared as my life was spiralling out of control, I did not know what to do except pray. I was so afraid that I was going to become a casualty of my own depression.

When I look back on that period in my life I feel I attracted everything negative that happened to me by worrying about money and my business over a prolonged period.

It all stemmed from a few years previous where I received my one only ever card reading (which was tarot). I was with a group of people who read the tarot cards on a regular basis and they persuaded me to have a reading. There were nine of us around the table and I was the last one to have a reading. As the cards were being turned over all of the laughing and joking stopped in an instant, each one looked at each other and then me and they tried to dismiss the cards as if there was not a problem.

However I knew they were being economical with the truth and explained that I am honest and open to things and expect the same in return. Eventually they explained that two of the cards read that everything would go and when I say everything I mean everything, my

Over the next few days all I could think of was losing everything; this turned to weeks, months, years until it was affecting all parts of my life.

Through these hard times my constant negative worrying ate into me like a cancer; if it was not for the love of my immediate family and a couple of very dear friends I dread to think what actions I would have sort to escape the torment

The inevitable happened my business folded I was personally declared bankrupt which resulted in my beautiful house being repossessed, I was now homeless and had to find a house to rent which was not a problem but finding a deposit was; fortunately a friend lent me the money for a deposit and we moved into a small house in a small town five miles away from my previous home.

Once things had settled down after a couple of months we felt it was time to lick our wounds and try to bring a little order to the chaos that we called our lives.

During this time I recalled a book I read in the 70's which included sections on how to create reality with your thoughts. I realised that yes I had a terrible couple of years but that period was now behind me and there was no way I could change what had happened in the past, but I can certainly affect what happens in the future.

This point in my life was a turning point and I realised the opportunity that was being offered to me; I began my affirmation journey with the simple affirmation "I am healed, thank you".

I knew that it took 21 days to break a habit and 30 days to form a new one and so began reciting my affirmation. At first I have to be honest here, it really didn't feel true, it was as though I was kidding myself however I persevered and after a week things began to change.

My partner found a new job, a friend loaned us a car and I also found a job within walking distance of our home. It was quite amazing how people, situations and general circumstances began to change.

When The Student Is Ready, the Teacher Shall Appear

Chinese Proverb

As positive things started to happen for myself and my family I began to get a warm glowing feeling as I practised my affirmations, you will find that even early on in your affirmations you will have a feel good feeling when practising your affirmations.

After the third week the affirmations were believable and definitely flowing easier from my mouth, mind and heart, I was becoming exactly what my affirmation said "I am healed, thank you" it felt as though I was beginning to step from under a massive dark cloud and seeing some light finally.

I know now that in the past my negative thoughts were overpowering my positive ones, so much so that I in the end allowed my negative thoughts to win and bring me financial ruin and despair.

I may have let those negative thoughts win that battle but I was not going to let them win the war. Did you realise that on average the human brain processes 60,000 thoughts in a day? The secret to success and fulfilment is not allowing your negative thoughts to overpower your positive ones. In the past I was probably thinking 95% + negatively; so what chance did my positive thoughts have against that!

We need to be tipping the balance the other way and have your positive thoughts overcome your negative thoughts which will then in turn influence your sub conscious mind. As you start with your affirmations you will still have negative thoughts it is impossible not to, but as long as you stick with the discipline of your affirmations several times a day every day for 30 days you will be tipping the balance towards the positive that much further each day. Remember once we have tipped the balance to just 51% of our thoughts that are positive to 49% negative then as in everything in life your positive thoughts will win the day.

Of course we do not want to stop when we get to 51% we have to keep going, this is a life changing process so we have to commit to this process long term; if you start your affirmations today you will look back on today as being the day you stood up to your bullying negative thoughts and replaced them with positive goal achieving thoughts.

As I carried on with my affirmations I also began recording them in a beautiful silk journal a friend bought me for Christmas. Whilst reciting your affirmations you will find it is greatly enhanced by writing the affirmation down in a journal.

After four weeks of working and performing my one affirmation for what felt like a thousand times a day as well as writing the affirmation down in a journal, I started to have these strange feelings about three or four inches above my navel, it felt strange, however nice.

These warm comforting feelings are what you will experience the more you practise your affirmations, some people describe it as a feel good feeling it is actually the excitement you are feeling as your affirmations are replacing the negative thoughts into positive ones and in turn your sub conscious mind is relaying the affirmation to the rest of your body which then results in the manifestation of the affirmation.

As my positive thoughts were starting to overpower my negative thoughts; people I had not seen for a while would stop me in the street and comment how well I looked and that I always had a smile on my face. I knew the affirmations were getting more powerful which gave me the confidence to add another affirmation "I have unlimited, health wealth and happiness and for that I am grateful". I knew the key to affirmations was to pay attention to how I physically felt when I spoke my affirmation and to try to generate that fuzzy feeling in my tummy.

My life has literally changed for the better, I am happy, healthy, and very blessed beyond my wildest dreams, however no one else has done this for me except me and therefore no else can change your life only you. I am not writing about anything that I have not experienced myself; these teachings come from my own personal experiences and I therefore know that they work if followed correctly.

WHY AFFIRMATIONS FAIL

For affirmations to effectively work they need to be spoken and written down with emotion, if you just scribble down the affirmations while chatting to a friend on the phone or recite them while watching your favourite soap on TV you are greatly diluting the potential of affirmations you will not realise the benefit and you will lose heart.

If you do not fuel your affirmations with emotion it will be the same result as not putting fuel in a car ...... you will not go anywhere!

If you are simply reciting your affirmations without emotion, then the affirmation becomes a boring routine and to the subconscious mind unbelievable and therefore a pointless waste of time.

Once we fuel our affirmations with emotion and intention, we are changing our inner world, which in turn mirrors it into our reality and therefore changes our outer world.

Let's say that you are affirming 'I am lovable', however you are thinking that you are not loveable and have no one in your life that loves you then this affirmation will not work!

If you affirm 'I AM LOVEABLE' with true self-belief that you are loveable and believe this to be so and also fuel it with emotion of being loveable, you are radiating energy that is fuelled with passion and therefore convincing the subconscious mind that this is true!

If you are not willing to believe what you are affirming, then there is no point in doing it.

Remember if the sub conscious mind thinks that you are not loveable and that no one will love you we have to tip the balance that you positively are loveable and yes people do love you or that a person out there WILL fall in love with YOU!

If you are not feeling on top form, and experiencing self defeating thoughts, there is no point in affirming anything because you simply will not gain anything from them.

For the affirmations to be effective they have to be specific and definite and have to be repeated with intention, awareness, sincerity, belief, desire and above all else emotion

Another common mistake is that people do not recite/write their affirmations in the present tense. You have to write in the present tense it is essential to the success of your affirmation

E.g. 'I HAVE financial freedom, thank you' NOT 'I NEED financial freedom, thank you'.

Your subconscious mind needs to think you are having financial freedom now so it will supply it NOW, if you state you need financial freedom then your sub conscious mind will leave you NEEDING!

If you are determined to make changes in your life, you need to be ready to release the past, just let it go, you certainly cannot change the past however you can change how you view it. Do not hang on to the past good or bad forgive yourself and others and start your affirmations as though you have turned over a new leaf.

When you affirm out loud, in your head or writing it down, feel excited and more than anything feel emotion, because if you are unemotional your words will definitely not convince the subconscious mind.

Once your subconscious mind is convinced by your thoughts, spoken affirmations or writings which are fuelled with emotion and belief, then and only then will it begin to bring about results.

Fuel your thoughts, words and writings with deliberate intention.

Choose your affirmations well, as a well chosen affirmation can ignite within you a new positive state of being.

When your affirmation is in the present tense,
"I am so lucky and grateful"
"I am so healthy"
"I have financial freedom, thank you"
- you will in effect begin to create a shift in your reality immediately.

It is best if you can see in your mind's eye an image of what you are affirming (if it is a watch, cut out a picture of it and keep it in your journal and look at it before you begin affirming, then close your eyes and see it in your mind's eye, feel it on your wrist) as it becomes more real and achievable.

Your affirmations have to be believable if they are going to work. If you feel uncomfortable speaking an affirmation, or if you feel that you are lying to yourself, then simply select a new affirmation, one that feels comfortable and begin the process again.

It is important that you recite your affirmations as often as you possibly can. Recite them at least six times in a row, morning, noon and night. The very last thing you must do before you drift off to sleep is to repeat them several times whilst seeing in your mind's eye what your desire and how wonderful you will feel when it is in your reality.

Writing my affirmations on a piece of paper and keeping them with me at all times, including keeping them under my pillow whilst sleeping works as I am consciously aware of them.

Many of my clients have their affirmations as their screensaver on their computer, you can have them on your mobile phone and if you set the alarm on your mobile it will remind you to recite them or write them down. Others put them on their fridge door, on mirrors in fact anywhere that will remind you to affirm your new reality. "I have perfect health and unlimited wealth, thank you".

Health Affirmations...

✵

Thank you for my perfect health and unlimited well-being

✵

I vibrate perfect health and vitality, thank you

✵

Energy and health is constantly flowing
through my mind, body and aura, thank you

✵

I love and accept my perfect health and well being

✵

My life is healed because I love myself, thank you

✵

My mind, body and soul is forever nourished
with perfect health and well-being

✵

My cup of perfect health and well being
is full to over flowing, thank you

Wealth Affirmations...

✹
I have enriched prosperity in my life, thank you
✹
I am so grateful for my financial freedom, thank you
✹
I pay all my bills on time with love and gratitude, thank you
✹
My financial cup is brimming, thank you
✹
Wealth, health and abundance flows freely through me
✹
I allow the silver thread of prosperity
to run through me and around me
✹
I am open and receptive to wealth and abundance, thank you

Love Affirmations…

✵

I love and accept myself totally and for that I am grateful

✵

I deserve love in my mind, body and aura
and I accept it now, thank you

✵

I am loveable and desirable, thank you

✵

I radiate love to everyone and everything, thank you

✵

The love that I give out is returned to me tenfold, thank you

✵

I am so happy I have love in my life every day, thank you

✵

I attract unconditional love in my life constantly, thank you.

✵

My cup is over flowing with love, thank you

Self-Esteem Affirmations…

✺

I believe in myself to always do the right thing, thank you

✺

I express my confidence with dignity and grace, thank you

✺

I am a unique and creative being, thank you

✺

My confidence is over flowing, thank you

✺

I am filled with love for who I truly am, thank you

✺

I am open and receptive to my self belief that is constantly flowing into my life, thank you

✺

I am filled with love and laughter. I love life, thank you

We are not human beings on a spiritual journey.
We are spiritual beings on a human journey.
Stephen Covey

CHAPTER NINE
THE UNIVERSAL LAWS

Are you aware of the universal laws working in your life every moment?

Universal laws are around us all of the time and they reveal themselves in all ways and areas of our lives, physically and also spiritually. The laws are constants and therefore understanding the laws is paramount to your success as you need to align yourself with these natural laws and certainly not work against them.

Stop for a moment and notice how the following universal laws are working in your life at the present time. There may be things that you would wish to adjust in your life right now. It could be your relationship, or maybe the lack of a relationship or the relationship that you are in is an unhappy one. It maybe that you would love a career change or in fact have a career. Do you feel happy and content? Maybe you would like your own home or a new car, in fact you may wish for many things to be changed in your life.

Everything in your life that has happened to you up to now or what will happen in the future is down to you by way of your beliefs, the thoughts that you think through the manifestation of the subconscious mind and the laws of the universe at work.

The universal laws are immutable and unchangeable which are powerful and can have damaging effects for those who do not understand them. In order of living a great life creating happiness and prosperity, we need to know the basic rules of how the universal laws work. When you understand the laws principles and use them intentionally, you are heading on the right track.

You are the co-creator of your life, however you have the power to turn things around by working and understanding the universal laws, you can be a conscious co-creator of your life! As co-creators, at times we have our 'victim blinkers' on and therefore do not always see the big picture as it actually is.

The first step is to take off the 'victim blinkers' and know that YOU are creating your life and the circumstances in it. If we do not like what we have created in the past then we can change it by creating the things we wish for now and into the future. It is not enough to have a thought; you need to direct it with your energy and intention. Once you know what you desire the best way to manifest it into reality is through visualisation, meditation and repetition.

The Universe will always mirror back to you what you radiate into it. If things in your life are not what you would like it to be then it could be that you are sending out mixed signals. The Universe will always and I mean always reflect back to you what you are offering through the expression of thoughts, words, feelings or actions. Let us look at it this way if you are asking the universe for love in your life by the way of a partner and you do not offer kindness or love to others then the Universe will reflect back to you exactly what you have sent out, therefore you will receive a partner, however probably an un-loving one.

By understanding the laws and how the laws work together, you can start to take an active role in understanding them and working with them. It is important that you simply do not sit back and let things happen in life. By taking responsibility for your life and actively taking interest and working with the universal laws you will develop into the co-creator of our your own reality.

I know how hard things can be and therefore know that anyone can improve themselves and their lives by having more optimistic attitude towards life. It is essential that you work within the rules. The rules of engagement establish what information is specified, at what time, to whom, and in what manner.

The universal laws are no different, knowing how the laws work is necessary to creating a life for you that is unlimited, meaningful and happy.

THE LAW OF LLOWING

This law is truly amazing and yet not the easiest law to take on board and understand, once you get to grips with it and master it, you will never look back. It is of great importance that you understand this law and how it works, however you will need to understand the law of attraction and the law of creation too. You are a co-creator and therefore responsible for your own creative process, your creative process dictates the result of your life.

You can be the master of your very own universe by mastering the law of allowing through being consciously aware. When you are consciously aware of your thoughts you are more in control of your lives. Being consciously aware is having intense focus, concentration and belief of turning your dreams into reality. What you have in your life now is a direct result of your thoughts and intentions.

The law of allowing is all about releasing our influencing control over our life, by this I mean anxiety, stress, fear, and so many other unconstructive emotions. Allowing is releasing the needing, the anxiety, the stress, the fear, the desiring, and the control and merely allowing your dreams and desires to be manifested by universal energies.

It is important to identify that we all have the ability to manifest our desires, however we have to allow ourselves to release and let go, furthermore you have to believe that you will actually receive them. The Garden of Release and Let Go is brilliant for this law. Being consciously selective about what you desire, and remember the old chestnut of whatever you place your focus on is what you will attract. Being able to control your thoughts is another step to becoming the master of your universe, then if you can simplify how you desire your life and its experiences to be through your thoughts you will no doubt attract the experiences that you wish for.

Your job is to discover what you desire, get into the flow of feeling you have your desire now and then allow it to flow into your life!

If you allow the law of allowing to work for you and by you not resisting, you will receive your dreams and desires. I know some of you will be thinking that you have done the creation part, however nothing is happening.

I know that is how I used to feel, you see when we put our desires out into the universe and our desires are not coming fast enough, or you try to reason with yourself how it will come and how will it happen, you are essentially expressing to the universe that you really do not trust that it will happen.

You doubt the length of time it is taking the universe to deliver it to you, or you doubt the process.

Hey presto, because you have doubted consequently you have just deleted your desire. It is vital that you understand this part, when you doubt or question the universe in how it will deliver your desire you in fact doubt our creator, our universe and its ability to accomplish your desires!

SUMMARY

The law of allowing will work for you if you simply allow it to.

Release any resistance you may have just let it go. Resisting is persisting. Having no resistance your energy will flow easily and constantly. By releasing any resistance you are allowing the universe to direct you one step at a time towards what you truly desire.

You trust the universe and expect miracles flow into your life all the time. You can make your life as simple or as difficult as you wish it to be.

Make your life simple by allowing and dance the dance of empowerment.

Life is NOT a dress rehearsal

THE LAW OF
DELIBERATE CREATION

The law of deliberate creation states that when we desire something and focus our thoughts on our desires as often as possible and our focus is with positive emotion and also with trust that we deserve our desire we can then accomplish our desire far faster.

When we think about our lives and everything that we have ever experienced, we have manifested and attracted our experiences by way of our thoughts, emotions and beliefs. I know for a fact that no one and that includes me wishes to believe that they are directly accountable for some of the unpleasant things that have happened in their lives.

Nonetheless, knowing that we are creators of our very own universe is a very sobering fact, which in a way is a positive thing.

When and only when we begin to take actual responsibility for all of our creations can we deliberately manifest the life that we aspire to. Therefore it is our thoughts that control our lives that control our emotions and it is our emotions that control our vibrational frequency.

When I used to worry all of the time, usually about money, or should I say the lack of it , I found that I was on a never ending cycle of lacking money simply because my thoughts and feelings were focused on lack. As these thoughts began to build momentum fuelled with emotions and feelings of lack, my mind became a mental snowball gathering impetus and going downhill rapidly.

I was affected in so many ways and my snowball just seemed to gather more speed, getting bigger and bigger, affecting not only my performance but also my behaviour.

Which literally was ruining my life, I really did not see any solutions or a way out, however eventually I learnt that we have choices; we have so many choices that are unlimited to us, it is all about making the right choices.

Key Point...

So, if something does not feel good from your viewpoint, why not look at it another way until it does feel good?

Create your reality that you are happy and comfortable with, that suits you. Having conscious thoughts of abundance and prosperity, attract thoughts and circumstances of a like kind. Having a conscious awareness and becoming one with your thoughts, words and emotions is what the law of deliberate creation is all about.

You are a deliberate co-creator of your life and you have available infinite power within you.

You can be, do and have whatever your heart desires!

The law of deliberate creation is conscious awareness of how we create our lives, accepting our personal unlimited power and using it to create the life of our dreams.

> If you want a quality,
> act as if you already had it.
> William Jones

EXERCISE

For this exercise you will require a clean piece of paper
with a line drawn down the centre.

At the top of the left hand side of the page write do not desire,
and on the right hand side of the page write my true desires.

In order of living the life of your dreams, you have to decide
what you really desire in your life.

Now to my way of thinking the only way of discovering this is by
writing down. (Writing it down is a way of it happening!)

In the left half of the page write down the things that you do not
desire, it can be anything, debt, unhappiness, lacking in confidence,
not having a car, loneliness, no home it is up to you what you write
down and how many you write down, however be honest with yourself,
as the only person in this equation is you.

Now on the opposite side of the page turn what is on the left hand
side around by one hundred and eighty degrees;
by turning it around you have discovered what you do desire.

It is imperative that you focus on what you really desire
as opposed to what you do not desire when creating.

A SAMPLE PAGE...

Don't Desire	Do Desire
I do not desire to be unhealthy and unwell	I desire to be healthy and brimming with good health
I do not desire to be poor and always lacking in money	I desire and deserve to have wealth and financial freedom
I do not desire to be fat	I desire to look slim and healthy
I do not desire being a couch potato	I desire to exercise and be healthy
I do not desire to be lonely, living on my own	I desire t have a partner in my life, living together happily
I do not desire to work where I work	I desire to have the perfect career change
I do not desire travelling on the bus	I desire to have a car to drive myself around

Having a clear view of your desires is the key to you becoming a conscious deliberate creator.

Now that you have discovered and are consciously aware about what your desires are, try to eliminate any negative self talk and wording. When you state your desires, whether verbally, written or in your mind.

It essential that you eliminate negative wordings; by this I mean specifically the words no, not and do not; these have to be removed from your language. Let us say that you desire to have a partner in your life, there is no point in stating that "you don't desire a man that is short and bald" as you are five foot ten inches tall, that does not make one iota of difference to the subconscious mind, all the subconscious mind thinks is you do not desire a man.

What you ought to be stating is "I desire a man who is six foot tall, with a full head of hair".

The key to successful deliberate creation is about developing clear mental images of what we do desire. You are the only one in your life that has complete control over all of your experiences.

Be consciously aware by having deliberate intentions of creating your desires and dreams in life. If we follow our desires on purpose, with top notch intention (intention is vitally important) of being the best of the best that you possibly can be, achieving wealth, health, prosperity and success.

The road leading to a goal
does not separate you from the destination;
it is essentially a part of it.
Charles De-Lint

To enable you to remain focused on deliberately creating, be conscious of your thoughts on a regular basis throughout your day. If you are able to, set your alarm on your phone for it to remind you, you can centre yourself and gather your thoughts at the designated times.

Notice your thoughts, are your thoughts optimistic and moving you forward towards your desires? Or, are they unstructured and holding you back? Remember that your thoughts and emotions are energy in motion. The more optimistic thoughts that you have will move you towards your desire, whilst on the other side of the coin the negative thoughts will hold you back and keep you stuck.

Think of a time when things were going wrong all of the time, and you could not see the wood for the trees that time might be now. If you can explore your thoughts past and present and how you conducted yourself at that time, you will discover that your negative thinking around those experiences was indeed very strong!

Now then, if these predominant thoughts became paramount and continually repeated in your mind over and over again, (which they more than likely did) they will have become your main way of thinking, autopilot, and an automatic negative reaction to how you perceive life.

In one respect daydreaming can be a wonderful thing, however on the other hand if your daydreaming is constantly repaying the same old negative thoughts over and over again you are on the hamsters wheel of allowing your thoughts to control you in a negative way.

You are unconsciously daydreaming on automatic pilot in a negative way which then results in your life automatically reacting to life in a negative way. The problem here is you are literally drawing your daydreams (or should I say nightmares) towards you at great speed, a little like the snowball gathering momentum downhill and the snowball becoming larger and larger!

We need to melt away that negative snowball and replace it with a runaway positive one which will then sculpture your life in a positive manner!

THE LAW OF VIBRATION

All that we are is the result of what we have thought.
Buddha

The law of vibration states that vibrations of specific frequencies are attracted to other vibrations of the same frequency. You offer a vibration out into the universe; the universe then matches that frequency and reflects it back to you.

The Law of vibration is one of the many universal laws that govern our universe and existence and is powerfully connected to the law of attraction. Everything in the universe is energy and the law of vibration states that no matter what it may be, it is energy. Your vibrational frequency sets the quality for your life.

We are all connected to the universal consciousness and to each other.

We are all vibrational energy beings.

Energy is constantly vibrating, it never stops. The Law of Vibration like all of the other laws is constant it never stops working, whether we choose to believe it or not. We do not always see the connection with it, but it is there. Everything vibrates at different rates or speeds.

Our thoughts have been proven to have different vibrations. Each thought vibrates at a specific frequency and through your own frequency you attract similar vibrating things into your reality.

Universal energy moves within us, all the way through us, and around us. It is vital that you are aware that we all have this power within us; and if learning to unleash this power you would greatly enhance your life and the lives of those around you.

When you pay attention to anything this means that you are placing your focus on it. The more attention (energy) that you give to a thought or a vision, then the vibration will gather speed and momentum.

The quicker the speed of vibration, the sooner it will be appear in the physical world.

Anything that you pay attention to or focus on will in effect move toward you and eventually materialise in your physical reality, likewise the more you have positive/negative thoughts these will in turn cause your positive vibrations to quicken in either a positive or negative way.

HOW TO USE VIBRATION

The law of vibration is strongly connected to the law of attraction.

The Law of vibration works for everyone in spite of being aware of this or not.

You attract things into your life with the thoughts and feelings

The law of vibration manifests to us in reality through the basis of the law of attraction.

Being consciously aware of vibrations is basically how you are feeling i.e. happy, sad.

Key Point...

Always remember that more often than not we acquire exactly what we expect, whether negative or positive. Thinking about this logically this is a very sobering thought and therefore if we live with that awareness we can create a dream life.

In order to receive all of the prosperity that you desire, you must be open and receptive by having faith that your desires are on their way.

You must continuously be aware of how you are vibrating and learn how to change the frequency from negative to positive, sad to happy, worry to freedom, tired to energetic, only you can change your frequency so get tuning your frequency now.

Unleash this inner potential by learning not to focus on the things you do not desire as in debt (as long as you believe and act like you are poor and struggling, then you will be), lack, loneliness, jealousy focus on what you do desire and not on what you do not desire.

It is essential that you observe yourself. As you think, feel and act, so you create the primary vibration of your being. This fundamental vibration then creates resonance with identical vibration frequencies in the universe. The result is an attraction of circumstances, people, challenges and opportunities in exact vibrational resonance with your own dominant vibration frequency.

SEVEN TIPS TO HELP YOU

To make positive changes in your life, you will need to think and radiate correct thoughts (vibrations). You will discover that things will change with discipline. It is not an instant, but gradual and with effort. You will begin to see things moving in an improved direction, in fact you may even be able to feel yourself "moving".

Always visualise a positive outcome no matter what.

Think about something that you desire (try something small to begin with, maybe a parking space) and then consciously focus all of your intention on what you desire.

See it in your life now, as though it is yours now, feel the sensations of happiness in your stomach now, similar to butterflies fluttering in your tummy. This concept is called "acting as if"; it is about having blind faith and believing in things that do not currently exist in your life. It is about embracing a new mindset and acting on your intention "of becoming".

Feel the success of having your desire now and act as if you already have it in your life now. Think about when you were a child you always believed that your dreams were real, and they were to you. Try to imagine that you can dream as you did when you were a child and generate that happy light hearted feeling of being carefree.

Take action by offering thanks in advance and write in your journal, 'thank you for my beautiful watch I am grateful for it, thank you'. Write this everyday as the way to make it appear in your physical reality.

Now simply let it go. You see you have to let go (you are not emotionally concerned in manifesting it) and during this process you allow it to manifest effortlessly. When you work with the law of vibration/attraction it is important not to make up a scenario where it leads to you receiving. You have to trust that The Universe will manifest to you.

THE LAW OF TTRACTION

I first came across the law of attraction in the mid seventies after reading the Seth book "The Nature of your personal reality" by Jane Roberts and "Bring out the magic in your mind" by Al Koran; I was very young then and quite impressionable and my word those books really made an impression on me.

Having worked with the law of attraction for a sometime, not only has it changed my life but also many of my clients to such a degree it is amazing. Understanding the law of attraction and the universal laws is paramount for you to be successful in order for you to receive everything that you desire in life. Your life can change almost overnight, it is all about knowledge of the universal laws and the subconscious mind, and you know the old cliché "knowledge is power".

You have the ability to raise and lower your vibration through your thoughts and feelings. To bring out your highest potential you should strive to live in a state of unconditional love, free of all judgements.

We have to realise that the law of attraction works intrinsically with many other laws and it is important to understand their unity.

Having studied the universal laws for many years, I have been able to consciously work with them to manifest my desires. Intention is the most important part of the manifesting process as it has to be for your highest good.

Your ability to manifest your desires into physical reality is guaranteed when you are in union with the universal laws and have free flowing strong positive energy. Each and every one of us holds the key to releasing our creativity to accomplish our dreams and desires; it is all about the power of intention.

> *Your personal point of power is right now, live, laugh and love!*
> Grace Brown

Key Point...

One of my tutors used a great analogy regarding thought.

He explained that by throwing a pebble in a pond it creates ripples; the ripples can be positive or negative.

The ripples will resonate with certain things in the pond and therefore will attract them.

Now, thought is no different as thought produces ripples.

So, are your thought ripples going to be positive?

If they are then you will certainly attract a more positive lifestyle.

One can choose to go back toward safety
or forward toward growth.
Growth must be chosen again and again;
fear must be overcome again and again.
Abraham Maslow

HOW TO USE THE LAW OF ATTRACTION

The law of attraction will always respond to how you are vibrating.

Your vibrations are literally like a frequency that the universe picks up and mirrors back to you something of a vibrational match.
It picks the vibration of your emotion that you are feeling and matches it with more of what is of the same frequency as your energy signal.

Your emotions are essential to what you are attracting with the Law of Attraction.

Being aware of your emotions and feelings gives you an indication to what vibrational state you are in at any given moment.

Manifesting is an in-built power everyone has.

The reason that we struggle to make changes in our lives is that the conscious mind has influenced the subconscious; and the problem there in is that your conscious mind does not control your belief system or your behaviour this is controlled by the subconscious mind.

Your conscious mind can reprogram the subconscious mind subliminally.

For many people, reprogramming the subconscious mind is relentless. Unfortunately, we engage ourselves in a lot of self sabotaging negative talk.

I cannot afford that or I am not clever enough to do that or he/she will not fancy me.... does this sound familiar to you?

Well, my teachings and exercises will help you.

Turn the negative into a positive
Grace Brown

CREATE YOUR DESIRE BY 'ACTING AS IF'

The acting-as-if technique is brilliant for working on your dreams and desires. Acting-as-if is where you act as if you have already achieved your dream or desire.

This technique works because it actually programs the subconscious mind to respond differently. When you are trying to manifest something you desire something that you do not have at present; your vibration will be incompatible with your desire as it is not familiar with that type of vibration.

When you act as if you already have your desire, your vibration will move into the frequency for you to manifest your desire into your reality. Acting as if we have achieved the manifestation of our desire, we activate within us a vibration that is compatible with its actual manifestation into our physical reality, and so effectively kidding our subconscious mind that this is the case.

'Acting as if' works in a number of different ways. Dwelling on the negative makes people feel worse. Acting as if things were how you would like them to be takes your focus off what is lacking and encourages you to focus on the positive. It takes your focus off yourself and puts it more on the relationship and the other person. This makes you feel better whatever else is happening.

HOW TO ACT 'AS IF'

When you enter into the world of acting as if, you will not be constantly attempting to make changes, you will really be making positive changes.

Acting as if focuses positive change within you.

Acting as if your life is how you would wish it to be, you are effectively living the life you truly desire.

Live your life in the present moment by acting as if you are already in possession of your desire.

Key Point...

If your desire is to have financial freedom, act as if you have that financial freedom.

What would you feel like if you won on the premium bonds or the lottery ...... yes you can feel that excitement in your tummy, the smile breaking out on your face the high pitch scream at the realisation of your massive good fortune, the running to tell your friends and family, checking the numbers not once, twice but ten times to make sure you have not made a mistake, do you go public or do you keep it a secret?

As I am writing this I can feel my vibration changing at the excitement of this happening!

This is what you must do several times a day everyday with passion and belief, because everybody has the energy to make this happen.

Everything comes into your life according
to the laws of attraction and divine timing,
when the time is right, and not until the time is right.
Grace Brown

CHANGING HOW YOU VIBRATE

There are two types of vibrations the first is positive and the second is negative. Now every single moment you are offering the universe your vibrations and your vibration comes from the thoughts you think and how you are feeling in that moment.

So let us use an example; the post man delivers your mail and you are having money problems and you see that there are some bills in your mail before you open the mail your tummy does a summersault and you begin feeling very anxious, and then you open the mail and you let out a groan....

That is you sending out your negative vibration; the law of attraction duly obliges and always responds and matches the vibrations that you offered in that moment.

> We are constantly sending out vibrations through our thoughts and our feelings.

JUDY'S PERSONAL EXPERIENCE OF ATTRACTING THE MAN OF HER DREAMS

In August 2006, I received a phone call from a lady wishing to make an appointment; she was specific with her questions about my practice and qualifications; happy with my answers Judy arranged an appointment for the following week.

I try to be generous with my time and on an initial consultation I usually allow around two hours; thirty minutes for form filling, thirty minutes generally finding out where they are in their lives at that present time along with any illnesses or injuries they may suffer from followed by a one hour treatment.

When Judy arrived she was quiet and a little shy, however the two hours flew and she promised to let me know how she felt the following week. The next morning she called me to say that she felt amazing and that she had slept so well and could she book another appointment for the following week.

After three weeks of treatments which included healing to her mind body and soul by the way of reiki, crystal and colour healing Judy began feeling well, had lots more energy and her confidence was beginning to return, so much so that she asked could I help her with her mission.

I was a little puzzled, however I said if I can I will; she proceeded to explain that she felt ready for some male company.

Judy and her husband had been separated and divorced for over two years, she lived alone with her little son aged 3, as she had not been on a date for years she felt completely out of her depth.

She knew I practised 'law of attraction' and wondered if I could help her to find a partner.

The following first week in September Judy arrived for her appointment very excited and raring to go.

One of the things we worked on initially during our previous sessions was to get Judy to begin to like herself, this may seem strange to you but when we met I soon realised that Judy didn't particularly like herself let alone love herself. One of the biggest problems in the world today is a lack of self-love.

Every relationship we have mirrors back to us and the love that we feel for ourselves.

When I say love yourself, what I mean is to accept yourself as you are, warts and all as no one is perfect, believe in yourself, trust in yourself, respect yourself and be kind to yourself.

How can you expect someone to love you if you do not love yourself?

How can you gain respect from someone if you do not respect yourself?

How can you make someone happy if you are not happy within yourself?

You have to be grateful for who you are and accept responsibility for who you are. Learn to firstly accept yourself for whom and what you are, this may be difficult as some people have a very low self esteem which may have been built up over years.

The problem I find with people with very low self esteem is that they cannot see the wood for the trees.

They assume everybody is perfect and that they are the complete opposite.

I have never met anybody who is perfect, they do not exist, everybody has good and bad points and it is just a matter of how you and others view these points.

I asked Judy to write down on one side of a piece of paper all her negative points in her eyes and all her positive points.

Negative Points	Positive Points
Unattractive	Kind Hearted
Over Weight	Sense of Humour
Single Mum	Beautiful Son
Unworthy	Owned her own home
Frumpy	Great Friends
	Good Job
	Car owner
	No real financial worries
	Close Family

So, we then looked at the list, firstly the positive list is longer than the negative list, in fact it could have been much longer as we were struggling for the negatives.

When you write down things in black and white you start to clear away the wood from the trees syndrome and see things as they are in a much clearer fashion.

In fact, I am sure most people reading this think that Judy has a lot going for her and funnily enough when she looked at the list she admitted the same. When you add in that she was not unattractive and her idea of overweight was a size 12 or possibly a squeeze into a size 10; then her list was heavily weighted (excuse the pun) towards the positive.

So, the first thing everyone should do when commencing on a law of attraction journey is to discover what you really wish for, but also realise what you have already and be grateful for it.

In using the law of attraction to attract love, you must have a clear vision of what you desire in your lasting relationship. I am talking specific details here, not generalisation. You see if you do not identify precisely what you desire, you could end up with another unhappy relationship.

So we began with a clean piece of A4 paper, I asked Judy to draw a line down the centre of the page and on left hand side of the page asked to write firstly seven things that she would not wish her man to be like.

You may wonder why I asked for seven; well I am a big believer in the power of seven, as all numbers have vibrations.

The Seven Wonders of the World, 7 is a mystical number, the number of flawlessness. Around the world, in all religions and cultures, the number 7 often appears within myths and legends and as a symbol of luck or power. The seven seas, seven dwarfs, seven days and seven deadly sins, I could go on forever.

JUDY'S LIST

NOT LIKE	LIKE
Short Man	6ft tall
Boring	Fun & Exciting
Baggage	Baggage Free
Lazy	Active
Unemployed	Employed
Skint	Solvent
Billie No Mates	Has fun friends

As you can see in Judy's NOT LIKE list, the list is understandable; in fact most people would not like those attributes in their partner either.

But, it is important to realise what we do not want in life to then be in a position to realise what we actually truly desire.

On Judy's positive LIKE list is was easy to put together as it was everything that was the opposite of what she had experienced in her previous marriage.

Judy was quite astounded and excited by the outcome of this little exercise as she really now knew what she desired in a man.

Through the contrast you gain clarity on what you desire to generate in your life.

Contrast creates clarity.

Knowing what you do not desire offers clarity for what you do desire in your life

I personally have had amazing success with this technique and many others have too. Her man was to be tall, full of fun and caring, free and single, active and agile with a good career and his own fun mates. Judy knew what she wished for in a relationship now I would guide her to the next step which is asking. Remember that each thought is an intention and your intentions become your reality. To think is to ask.

Judy asked are there limits for what you can ask for. There are certain boundaries regarding what can be attracted, they are your boundaries of belief, not boundaries of what can potentially be attracted. You will only attract what you perceive to be true through your beliefs, so if you feel unworthy or unlovable, then sadly you will not receive your desire you will only receive what you feel you deserve which can be something much weaker or watered down.

Judy wrote in her journal everyday about her lovely man. She described him as kind, generous, funny and above all a very loveable man. I also advised Judy to make room for him in her home by leaving some wardrobe space for him, sleeping on one side of the bed leaving the other half for him.

She also moved her car to the end of her garage drive so he had room behind her car to park his. The thing that really struck a chord for me was that she began writing love letters to her new man; they were beautiful, funny, witty and sexy. Judy was really inviting love into her life on all levels of her being.

It was three months and nine days to when she encountered the love of her life. Judy had joined her best friend and her husband for a friend's birthday in town. When she arrived there were quite a few people there that she knew and dutifully went round everyone offering her best. Then she spotted this gorgeous guy that she had been manifesting leaning on the bar speaking to her best friend Angela. She walked over and with butterflies in her tummy asked Angela and the lovely guy if they would like a drink and that was the moment that Judy's life changed.

They discovered they had both lived in the same town for their entire lives, literally only streets apart. Judy went to junior school with his best friend, and his best friend's sister at Beauty College. Even though they were both connected to some of the same friends throughout high school they had not met. They are now very happy together four and half years later, they never look back they only live in the NOW.

It does not matter what age you are or where you come from anyone can take advantage of the law of attraction.

You simply have to find what you do or don't want in life and put it into practice.

THE LAW OF ESONANCE

Everything that is present in the universe in effect exists within us. Resonance is not new to any of us it is something that everyone experiences all of the time, non-stop, the law of resonance never sleeps!

Vibrational resonance is created from your thoughts and feelings, as you emit a vibration that vibration will go out to The Universe and seek a vibrational match on the same frequency e.g. If you are worried about paying your gas bill, the vibrational resonance that you send out fuelled with that emotion will resonate with an identical match and mirrored back into your life resulting in not being able to pay the bill.

The law of resonance states that when one vibrating system comes into contact with another vibrating system, the vibration of the weaker system will lower its vibrational energy to match that of the stronger system. In other words, the vibration of the stronger system will adjust the energy of the weaker system.

We can all choose how we think and feel, we all have a choice and if we can recognise that we have that choice, and learn how to live consciously then we can decide how we desire our future to be. It is all down to how we allow ourselves to think and feel each moment!

When you make a decision to make changes to how you think and begin to think consciously this in turn creates a change in your energy system and therefore the vibrations or signals you are offering changes, which will bring to you new vibrational matches.

The Law of Resonance works side by side with the law of attraction.

Many people believe and accept that the law of attraction establishes what is attracted towards you into your life; however it simply states that you will attract something that you are placing your focus on. So the law of resonance is the law that decides what you will attract by what you are in fact offering vibrationally with your thoughts, feelings, emotions, actions and deeds

To become really powerful with the law of resonance you have to make it your best friend, ensuring that you centre all your attention on your good positive feelings. It is your feelings that are being transmitted to the Universe just like a radio signal.

Make sure that your intentions are firstly good, clear and strong because the stronger the signal then the easier it is for that the signal to be picked with a vibrational match. There is nowhere on this earth where the universe is not present, I am sure you have heard people say 'she or he is giving off bad vibes' or you might know someone who always ends up in a relationship with someone who always greatly lets them down.

Everything you see, do and say generates a vibrational resonance and is sent out into The Universe to find a vibrational match, work on making your vibrations completely positive.

I am very passionate that you understand that thoughts become things and that with each thought that you think, you are vibrationaly tuning in to a thought frequency.

As I explained earlier like a radio signal the law of attraction will tune into that signal and bring to you a vibrational match, corresponding to the things that your frequency is offering.

Always try and give off positive, optimistic thoughts; the more you do it the more it will become second nature and once this happens the law of attraction will naturally reciprocate in positive and optimistic ways.

Try following these tips because they make a difference as to how you vibrate and therefore how your life will develop.

If you can begin to be focused and optimistic you are on your way to consciously manifesting your desires to create a new life.

HOW TO USE RESONANCE

To create the life of your dreams it is essential that you keep
your vibration level as clear and as high as possible.

Gain clarity of thought and action by raising your energy levels
so that you feel good about yourself and your life.

Keep a clear head so you can lift up your spirits and keep them lifted

Steer clear of negative people; if you cannot avoid them simply spend as
little time with them as possible. It is important that the people you
spend time with are optimistic and positive in their outlook on life.

Do something different every day.

Move into the winning circles of friends that enjoy fun and laughter.

Live, laugh and love lots and lots.

Love yourself and moreover accept who you are, live each day as if it
is your last and enjoy the fruits of you creations. Affirm at least
ten times a day "I deserve the best", "I feel energised and powerful".

Treat yourself, do something especially for you something that
you can take pleasure in and make you feel good.
All of which will raise your vibrationary level.

Consciously feel and state for what you wish for and aspire to
and feel deep down inside your solar plexus that it is truly possible
and in the process of being created.
Feel it, now feel it even stronger within you, now,
and feel it within the very core of you that you have what you wish for.

Feeling is the secret key to everything!

THE LAW OF MIRRORS

The way you feel within will be mirrored into your personal reality as the universe will always mirror back what your vibrational offering is. To change something in your life, you must firstly change your thought processing.

The universe will always mirror what your beliefs are. A belief is a thought that you keep thinking and thoughts can be changed. The law of mirrors is exactly as it reads; it is universal law that mirrors back to you your beliefs of who you really are. It is constant and should not be ignored, and it knows everything.

Life is a mirror and everything you experience is a reflection of your true self. Your life and everything in it is a reflection of you.

When you stand in front of a mirror you can see a reflection of yourself in the mirror, that reflection is not really you it is a representation of the real you. The mirror represents you, it is a result.

Your circumstances in life are results. The only way that you can conquer what is being mirrored into your life is to change how you think because it is your thoughts that cause the situations in your life and therefore what is mirrored back into your life.

HOW TO USE THE LAW OF MIRRORS

To make changes in your life, change your thoughts and your thoughts will change your beliefs.

If the energy frequency you are emitting is not powerful enough then there will be little change.

In the woven tapestry of the universe your dreams and desires await you, go for that perfect reflection.

THE LAW OF

Cause & Effect

I know so many clients, friends and family that go through their lives making the same mistakes, following the same patterns, and thinking that what they have in life is their lot as they are unable to make any lasting changes.

The law of cause and effect states that our thought is the cause and the effect is its manifestation. The system of cause and effect includes everything within the universe and are the beginnings of all conditions past, present, and future. Everything first exists as a thought before you experience it in your life. It is important that you understand how the cause and effect law works to enable you to attain peace in your life.

Cause gives rise to effect. Each thought that we think, each word that is spoken, each action that we take is a cause that is fired off into the universal sea of energy, producing ripples of effects of either good or not so good. This law will always return to you, guaranteed, always, so therefore it is important that you understand fully what you are creating with your thoughts, words or actions.

My lovely mum always taught me as a child growing up "Do unto others as you would have them do to you". We have to realise and accept that we are responsible for what we think, say and do. When we are not thinking, speaking or acting consciously, our minds can be chaotic; the effects of this law will occur because we put it in motion. A cause (the thought, feeling or action) that is produced will always create its appropriate outcome.

You must always be conscious of what you are thinking, saying and doing. You are liable for the thoughts that you produce and the final effect of you own mind and wisdom. The working of the law of cause and effect include everything in the universe and is the beginning of all situations, past, present, and future.

If there is an unwanted effect in your life, whether it is lack of money, bad relationships, unsatisfying livelihood or any other difficulty, you can trace that effect back to the things that you have done that may have caused it and then by eliminating the causes you can start to remove the effects.

Key Point...

With the law of cause and effect, we are all subject to the laws precise effectiveness.

We are the only ones that can accept its effect; no one else can experience it for us, once the effects begin to unfold and are revealed to us.

You see we are responsible for the cause and therefore have to experience the effect. In other words you have to take responsibility for your thoughts, words and deeds.

Now that you are aware that you are a cause for everything in your life you can now begin take get a grip on your life!

Simple, it really is, it is all about reprogramming your mind.

> Shallow men believe in luck.
> Strong men believe in cause and effect.
> Ralph Waldo Emerson

VISUALISATION OF CAUSE AND EFFECT

Visualising is the process of generating images in your mind and is an effective tool that assists in controlling the power of your subconscious mind. I visualise first thing in the morning and just before bed, however, I am also visualising on and off all day.

You are probably thinking that this sounds difficult and that you do not have the time for this kind of commitment, it will not be easy at first, yet stick with it and watch the magic happen. By making this twice daily commitment you are fast tracking your way to your goals, dreams and desires.

It takes twenty one days to break a habit and thirty days to form a new one, so I would recommend that you focus on simply changing your thought patterns to begin with visualising a change in your thought processing.

See yourself as being happy and smiling, content, not judging others, free from stress or worry.

Try not to visualise massive changes in your life in the beginning.
Keep it simple.

The reason I say keep it simple is because when things begin to change you have to be ready to handle the change; it has to be gradual, simple baby steps. I am not saying do not reach for stars, I am basically saying let's learn to walk before trying to run.

Many of our thoughts are habitual and are literally unconscious thoughts. When we observe our thoughts it truly makes us stop and look at what we are thinking however it brings about a consciousness within us.

When you are visualising, you will gain great benefit from using a technique called conscious breathing, this is where you sit down in a calm and peaceful room and through breathing techniques your visualisation is greatly enhanced.

CONSCIOUS BREATHING TECHNIQUE

Firstly try ensuring that you have peace and quiet without any distractions, when I first started using this technique I used to use ear plugs to help me to concentrate. Now we are going begin with a little conscious breathing. It takes practice to develop good breathing habits; you know the old cliché "practice makes perfect".

1...

Sit comfortably. I like to sit up because I will not go to sleep sitting up; keep your spine straight and your chest up. Relax for a couple of minutes.

2...

Start by relaxing the muscles of your feet, calves, thighs, stomach, chest and shoulders and finally your arms, relaxing all of your muscles and allowing all tensions to move out of your body. If any thoughts or images come into your mind do not pay them any attention, simply let them go.

3...

Close your eyes and breathe in slowly through your nose (if you cannot breathe through your nose for some reason then breathe through your mouth) for four counts, hold for four counts and then release through your mouth one, two, three and four and then repeat six times.

You will probably feel quite different and possibly a little light headed. However after your first few times you will start to feel relaxed. You will begin to look forward to your conscious breathing as you will be feeling its positive effects and in general its therapeutic properties, I can definitely say that for me breathing consciously is unquestionably a great healing tool.

4...

So now whilst you are breathing try to see in your mind's eye, yourself consciously seeing your desire and smiling. Focus on your desire intensely e.g. if your desire is a brand new car – see the car, imagine the smell of the leather upholstery, hear the engine, see yourself sitting in the car, see yourself driving the car with a smile on your face.

The more you practise this technique the more powerful the images will become in your mind. Eventually, your subconscious mind will assume the car is part of your life and working with The Universe will manifest it into your life.

THE LAW OF ANIFESTATION

The law of manifestation is in union with our thoughts. As I stated previously our subconscious mind creates our reality from the thoughts that we think and the beliefs that we accept as true.

Manifestation only begins when your mind is open and receptive to receive. Manifestation only begins when you are in the right frame of mind.

It is your subconscious mind that creates your reality.

It accepts the instructions the conscious mind offers (the conscious mind understands what is real) and then manifests into your reality. The instructions consequently go in the form of one's beliefs and thoughts.

THE LAW OF

The 'NOW' is the most important moment because the past has gone and cannot be changed and the future has yet to happen.

Only NOW MATTERS as life is a chain of NOWs.

You are a different person NOW than you were yesterday because your experiences of the last 24 hours will have changed you.

You cannot know who you will be in 'the future'; live only for NOW and you will see that almost all your stress, worry, fear and negativity is not here NOW!

THE LAW OF  ALLOWING

The law of allowing is about changing your thoughts...

You have for years acquired beliefs that are literally implanted into your subconscious.

You have to change those subconscious thoughts.

By doing this you are telling your subconscious that you "allow" your desires into your life; this seems obvious but it is important that you allow the changes to take place.

CHAPTER 10
WHAT YOU RESIST, PERSISTS

Because we are vibrational energy beings, we literally draw events and circumstances into our lives.

This is often the case when we resist change resulting in the problem persisting.

The more that we focus our attention on something, then the stronger our vibration becomes, therefore the faster it will manifest in our life.eg if you constantly worry about being overweight, you are in fact resisting change by thinking about being overweight and your obesity will persist.

RESISTANCE

When we push against something, it will push back against you.

I know from personal experience that the more you place resistance on something, that something will literally keep raising its ugly head and in some cases it can even get worse.

When we resist, we are not accepting something.

Many people are unaware of this and are often unaware of when or what they are resisting.

Whenever you find that things are repeatedly happening in your life that makes you feel uncomfortable you are in fact resisting.

When you resist something, whatever you are resisting will continue and therefore consequently you will keep re-living it over and over again, until you finally face whatever it is and deal with it, therefore putting it to rest.

SARAH'S TALE

One of my clients Sarah kept focusing on never having any money, things were continuously going wrong for her in her life, her life was a shambles.

I tried to help her to see that she was constantly inviting more 'lack' into her life, what she was resisting had to keep persisting in her life.

Once she also understood how the process works she began writing her resistances down on paper and things began to happen, she became quite uninterested in her lack and started making plans for her future by setting intermediate goals.

What she did in effect was stop the inner chatter of her mind and not pay any attention to her situation mentally and emotionally, her situation of lack began to fade away.

You may find that past events play tricks on your mind where that little something keeps popping into your mind?

Now for you to be able to prevent this situation or feeling, you will have to control your mind. The mind really does not like any form of discipline and therefore will refuse to accept any effort on your part to take any control over it.

Due to the mind loving its freedom, you will discover at first that it will be difficult to control your mind.

It will stand its ground and stand in your way of you gaining control, in some cases it will interrupt you, it will make you forget things at designated times, it will make you tired, it will do anything to stop you controlling it, however you must be strong if you wish to master your mind.

Let us say that you have had a desire for a quite some time without it manifesting itself, this would say to me that you have some sort of resistance to your desire that is stopping you from receiving it.

It is your thoughts, emotions, and beliefs that are not in union with what you are desiring, deep down within you there is doubt, you probably do not believe that you will receive it.

So let us have a look at some of the things that you maybe resisting.

DO YOU KNOW WHAT YOU ARE RESISTING

You are probably unconsciously resisting a specific outcome,
a particular set of events, or a certain feeling.

Your thoughts when fuelled with emotion will have a
massive impact on your world and everything in it,
good and not so good.

Allow your feeling to be your emotional guidance system.

If you feel abandoned and unloved, you are in fact
resisting love and adoration in your life.

When you think and feel "I really don't wish to feel sad and lonely",
sadly you are only attracting that very situation
of being sad and lonely into your life.

If you wish to surpass it you will need to
embrace everything and resist nothing.

You have to have control over your life and be free from resistance.
Being free of resistance means you have control of your mind.

A CLASHING OF THE OLD AND NEW YOU

A huge clash will take place within you, because the conscious mind does not like change.

HOW TO HANDLE CHANGE

Before you can bury this old to make way for the new, you have to face it head on and make peace with it.

Otherwise it will never rest in peace and you will never accept yourself totally and completely.

You are literally a magnet and you are attracting that which you are constantly placing your focus upon.

Change your thoughts and stop focusing on the things that you do not wish for, you will then stop resisting it and therefore stop manifesting it.

So you have to look adversity in the eye and face the adversities head on. Face them, experience them, face up to them and move on and rise above them and then and only then will you be free.

The negativity is part of your make up, by way of your belief system, a massive part of you that felt betrayed, discouraged and ill-advised.

You have to recognise and deal with them otherwise you are going to have a very miserable negative life and manifest everything that you really do not wish for!

3 TIPS FOR THE NEW YOU

Each and every time that you do not acknowledge them and resist them, they simply come back at you with even greater gusto.

It is all about your personal inner conflict, being in conflict with who you really are.

So many people believe that they are truly limited and yet they are the complete opposite, however due to their negative demons they believe it anyway.

BEING NON RESISTANT

By being none resistant in any given situation, event or circumstance you are releasing and diffusing the potential problem.

Let us say that someone has made you angry and you keep going over the same situation in your head reliving it and each time becoming angrier.

You more than likely want to fight fire with fire, you cannot, this is going to drive you mad, however you have to let go.

THE SECRETS OF CHANGE

You cannot change what happened but you can change how you view it.

Hold forgiveness in your heart and let go.
If you do not you are giving your potential problem power over you and you will be in the process of manifesting all sorts of negativity.

As I said earlier if you wish to be the master of your universe you have to release anger, aggression and retaliation and allow unconditional love into your heart, allow unconditional love to flow into and out of your body.

This maybe a challenge for you.

However give it a try...

...and watch the magic happen.

OTHER PEOPLE FOCUSING ON YOUR PROBLEM

When you are dealing with whatever problem you have in your life, refrain from sharing these problems with friends and family.

I know you have probably heard of the saying 'a problem shared is a problem halved' but actually if you share this information with others you in effect are multiplying the problem as more people will be focusing on that problem but in the wrong way.

3 STEPS OF SILENCE

We increase and bring into manifestation what
we collectively focus our thoughts and energy upon.

The more as a collective we resist something,
unfortunately the more it will persist.
It is human nature for people to gossip.

Keep your own council and maintain silence!

SUMMARY OF RESISTANCE

When we choose to resist something, we are in fact choosing for that something to persist.

Whatever energy you put out into the Universe, will come back to you like a boomerang.

If you find that circumstances, events and people begin appearing in your life that you do not desire and makes you feel uncomfortable, your natural instinct would of course be to resist it, to refuse it, and become upset and frustrated about the situation.

You need to learn to not be reactive as this reaction is ensuring the problem will persist

If you can grasp the concept that these things are enduring, you will have the power to create and not react.

CHAPTER ELEVEN
GRATITUDE

BEING IN A STATE OF GRATEFULNESS

A state of gratefulness is the golden thread of love that flows from your heart and permeates everything and everyone in The Universe.

The law of attraction is always in action and being in a state of gratefulness means that you will receive more things to be grateful for.

Gratefulness is the golden key to unlock the great resources of this bountiful universe bringing you health, wealth and abundance.

> Have gratefulness for your life
> and for the people who enrich your life
> with the golden thread of love.
> Grace Brown

THE POWER OF TWO LITTLE WORDS

The two little words of THANK YOU can make a huge difference to what you receive in your life. It also makes the people in your life feel heartfelt gratitude and feeling gratitude is the key to what is in your life at present.

If you can make the state of gratefulness your natural attitude, watch the magic happen.

Even when I write or speak my affirmations, I always add thank you on the end. The following affirmation encompasses everything, try it and see how you feel once you have recited it out loud five times.

> I am grateful for everything and everyone in my life,
> thank you, thank you, thank you.
> Grace Brown

HAVING GRATEFULNESS FOR THE CHALLENGES IN LIFE

If you have obstacles in your life be grateful that you are here to overcome them and see them as your stepping stones to your success. There is always something or someone to challenge us in life and essentially it is how we deal with those challenges that matters. Gratefulness can help you to learn from the challenges in life by making you a person with gratitude as your state of mind.

> **Counting your blessings is an art in the tapestry of life; begin weaving your gratefulness into this amazing tapestry of life now.**
> Grace Brown

COUNTING YOUR BLESSINGS

One...two...three...counting your blessings is a good habit to form. Counting your blessings is an act of gratefulness and gratefulness connects with positive emotions such as happiness, pleasure, and anticipation and is a powerful and effective technique if used on a daily basis.

Bing Crosby sang in the song "Count your blessings" When I'm worried and I cannot sleep, I count my blessings instead of sheep, and I fall asleep counting my blessings.

Try counting your blessings instead of sheep when you go to sleep and see what unfolds because when you sleep your subconscious mind continues working, in fact it never sleeps. The subconscious mind performs powerfully whilst the conscious mind is in the sleep state or when it is inactive.

> **Count your blessings instead of sheep.**
> Bing Crosby

Going to sleep with gratefulness in your heart you will awaken with positive grateful energy. If you write and speak five things you are grateful for before going to sleep you are re-programming your subconscious mind to perform the gratefulness whilst you sleep so your conscious mind cannot interfere.

However if you feel that before bedtime is not a good time for you then anytime you can will be good time to simply count your blessings, give thanks and be grateful for all that you have at least once a day.

I am grateful for my attitude of gratitude

Grace Brown

If the only prayer you said in your whole life was, "thank you," that would suffice.

Meister Eckhart

HOW TO USE THE LAW OF GRATITUDE

Establishing daily practice of gratitude and
writing them down is launching a new habit.

If you can set your alarm on your mobile phone to
remind you of your gratefulness for the same time each day.

Change your passwords on your computer to gratefulness or gratitude.

Put an image of the words gratefulness or gratitude
as a screen saver on your computer.

Every evening before going to sleep reflect, speak out loud
and write in your journal 5 things that you are grateful for.
Let your subconscious mind do the rest of the work while you sleep.

See in your mind's eye what you are grateful for;
feeling the emotion of gratefulness within you.

Be grateful for everything in your life,
the roof over your head,
the running water to take a shower or a bath,
the kettle you can boil to make a cup of tea,
the food on your table,
the bed you sleep in,
your health,
your friends and family
and basically everything and anything
that you may have taken for granted previously.

Show gratitude for new opportunities coming your way
and embrace them with joy.

Grace Brown

Chapter 12
De Cluttering Your Life

When I began my training in becoming a feng shui consultant it was made very aware to me by my tutors that clutter in any area of your home or life is a sign of energy that is stuck and stagnant. My tutor used to say that clutter was chaotic to our everyday living and as budding consultants we had to bring order to our chaotic lifestyle. You see the more clutter you have in the home, the more sluggish the energy will become.

If you have clutter in your home now, try this little exercise; walk into where your clutter is and stand there for several moments breathing in and out gently, now how do you feel being surrounded by all this clutter? Do you feel the air you are breathing in is stagnant and stale? Everything is energy and when the energy is obstructed and not flowing freely it becomes stagnant and stale, to simply remedy this de clutter every room in your home.

It is important to understand that clutter includes not just junk and rubbish but things you no longer have a use for as well as items you may have fallen out of love with; certain items can trigger memories of difficult or tough times in your life and in turn this will have a low complex energy that drains the living energy from you.

When your home is filled with clutter, it is very draining and therefore the very thought of where to begin can be quite overwhelming. But, the effort of de cluttering will give immediate results so try and break it down to a less over bearing challenge by de cluttering a room a day.

During your de cluttering process decide what items you want to keep, what to throw away, what to give to charity shops and even what you may be able to sell on auction websites like Ebay; it is all about getting rid of items and stuff that you do not need which in turn will unblock the energy resulting in it to begin flowing freely through your home.

Once you have decided to commence battle with your clutter you will feel the benefit immediately, however always remember clutter somehow has a way of sneaking into your home without being asked in and generally in the same areas over and over again so be vigilant and have a constant eye on the lookout for clutter.

Take the stress out of your life by simply organising such things as keys, coins, pens, lottery tickets and receipts because these are the things most often left cluttering tables and surfaces.

Once you have de cluttered your whole home including garages and sheds you will feel peaceful and positive, through your good work you will be ready sit back and enjoy your rewards of good health and good fortune.

AURAS

Your physical body is surrounded by an energy field known as the Aura, where your life force energy flows. The aura permeates and extends out past the physical body by several feet completely surrounding the body.

The aura itself is an oval shape and surrounds and encapsulates the life force energy acting as a sheath. Everyone and everything including animals, plants, and objects has its own unique aura.

Your aura is like a vacuum cleaner that sucks up every thought, word, feeling and action of your life and also mirrors your physical health, well-being, mental and emotional states.

Within the aura there seven main layers, these layers are your surface vehicles through life. Although there are seven layers we are going to concentrate on four of the layers within the aura; they are the physical, emotional, mental and the astral/spiritual layers all of which function at differing levels of frequency. The layers are your vehicles in life.

The aura comprises of an array of electromagnetic vibrations, the closer to the physical body the more dense the energy is, moving farther away from the physical body the energy within the layer becomes finer.

To the novice auras are not visible to the naked eye, but as you gain experience on how to view auras through the exercises provided you will begin to have success in viewing them starting with the closest layer to the physical body known as the etheric layer. The etheric layer is a pale bluish- grey mist reflecting your physical and emotional well-being, and the many obstacles affecting it.

The aura consists of all the colours and vibrations of the rainbow; colour affects the subtle flow of energies within the energy body. The aura responds to all kinds of colours including clothing, furnishings and food, in fact everything connected to colour. Colour plays a very large part in our emotions, soothing, invigorating or even agitating them.

THE ETHERIC LAYER - 1ST LAYER

The etheric layer is also known as the blueprint of the physical body. The etheric layer vibrates at a higher frequency than the physical body and is the key to your well-being.

Any illness or disease of the body will manifest itself firstly in the etheric layer before it shows up in the physical body as symptoms of the illness or disease.

This layer is susceptible to strong emotions like trauma, unprocessed emotions and shock; if this happens to you then your health and well-being will be under great duress.

3 FABULOUS ENERGY EXERCISES

Try the following energy exercises to establish your own personal energy.

During this exercise you will be asked to pull your hands apart (palms facing) like a fisherman exaggerating about the size of his catch.

Try this exercise every day or as much as possible, working with it daily you will begin to truly feel your energy getting stronger and stronger between your hands.

Quick Energy Exercise 1...

Take your thumb; either will do as you will do this on both hands now push the flat part of your thumb into the centre of your hand, hold it there for 30 seconds, whilst you are doing this close your eyes and feel the connection between your palm and your thumb.

Repeat again on the other hand.

For about 60 seconds quickly rub your hands together as though you are warming them on a freezing cold day

Very slowly and gently pull your hands apart (still facing each other) to approximately 8". Hold them there for 1 minute.

Very slowly and gently pull your hands further apart (still facing each other) to about 12", again hold this position for 1 minute.

Now push your hands back in slowly to 6" feeling the force between your hands, hold this position for 1 minute.

Pull your hands back out slowly to 12" again feeling the force between your hands, holding again for 1 minute.

Continue this process for about 10 minutes; you should be able to feel the energy building up between your hands!

Quick Energy Exercise 2...

❂

Push the flat part of your thumb into the centre of your other hand, hold it there for 30 seconds. Close your eyes and feel the connection between your palm and your thumb.
Repeat again on the other hand.

❂

For about 60 seconds quickly rub your hands together as though you are trying to warm them on a freezing cold day

❂

Take your dominant hand and begin holding your hand about 4" above your non-dominant shoulder for 1 minute.
(If you are righthanded, your non dominant shoulder is your left.)

❂

As you are holding your hand there you should be able to feel the energy between your hand and your shoulder.

❂

Begin slowly and gently moving your hand down towards your elbow, keeping a four inch gap between your hand and your arm.

❂

Can you feel the energy between your dominant hand and your arm? If you cannot with practice you will.
Can you feel the energy brushing your arm as your hand moves up and down? If you cannot with practice you will.

❂

Continue your elbow down to your fingertips, the more you practise this the more you will be able to feel your energy.

❂

Now repeat exactly the same on the other arm.

❂

Quick Energy Exercise 3...

For about 60 seconds quickly rub your hands together
as though you are trying to warm your hands
on a freezing cold day.

Keeping your eyes closed at all times
during exercise is important.

Slowly take your dominant hand and simply
place it 4" above your navel.

While holding your hand in that position, start to take deep
breaths to the count 4 and then breathe out to the count of 4,
and begin to feel the warmth under your hand.

Stay like this for 2 or 3 minutes, now very slowly remove
your hand from your stomach and take it to your face.

Your palm should be about 3" from your face,
now begin moving your hand around your face.

You will feel the motion of your dominant hand across
the surface of your face. It may be tingling or
it may be warm. If you cannot with practice you will.

Repeat with the other hand.

THE EMOTIONAL LAYER - 2ND LAYER

The emotional body encompasses every colour of the rainbow, when the emotional layer is of good health and well-being, its colour hues are stunning bright splodges of energy and colour. When you are experiencing feelings of love, happiness, pleasure, anticipation, then these are good emotions and means that you are processing, experiencing and feeling your emotions, therefore the colours will be vibrant.

At the other end of the scale is the emotions of anger, confusion, sadness, hurt, disillusion and trauma that will result in the emotions being un-processed and unreleased, these negative emotions would show as non vibrant colours.

The emotional layer stores every emotional experience from your life; principally the emotions that become stored are because they are not being processed, therefore in order to heal the emotions they should be worked through, recognised and released, leaving them in the past where they belong.

Try the quick emotional layer exercise opposite.

If whilst performing this exercise thoughts and images keep popping in to your mind, simply allow them to gently float off in a golden balloon of love.

Remember that you can repeat this exercise as often as you wish.

This emotional layer exercise is a great way to create inner harmony and self transformation within oneself.

Practicing 'I AM LOVE' brings your awareness right into the present moment, overflowing with love in the heart and emotional layer.

Emotional Layer Exercise...

✼

Find somewhere where you will not be disturbed for ten minutes.

✼

Sit with your back upright. Drop your shoulders, letting them to flop.

✼

Release the tightness in your jaw and allow your jaw to fall open.

✼

Now relax your tongue, allow it to relax.

✼

You should be feeling better already.

✼

Breathe in slowly (count of 4) On the 4th breath say I AM out loud.

✼

Hold it for the count of 4 slowly.

✼

Now breathe out slowly for the count of 4,
on the 4th breath say LOVE out loud.

✼

After repeating three times, take you dominant hand
and place it flat about 4 to 5 inches above your navel.

✼

Place your non-dominant hand it flat on the centre of your chest.

✼

Repeat the 'I AM LOVE' exercise for five minutes or longer.

✼

You will probably feel a little light headed,
however you will feel calm and serene.

✼

THE MENTAL LAYER - 3RD LAYER

The Mental Layer is connected to your thinking and thought processing. It is your manifesting layer and is therefore a very powerful layer. It encapsulates your thoughts, beliefs and ideas, consequently it is important that the thoughts you continually think are good, powerful and productive ones.

It is this layer where you not only think, you also reason and create. As well as these you also gather knowledge and information, through reason and logic.

Because this layer creates your reality the energy needs to be strong and clear if you are to experience well-being in all aspects of life. If your energy isn't strong then your energy levels will be running on empty and you will be feeling tired, deflated, listless and run down, finding it difficult to concentrate.

The colour associated with the mental layer is yellow, however if the thought is fuelled with emotion then colours from the emotional body will merge with the yellow.

Have you heard the saying or has anyone ever said to you 'that you look deep in thought'? It is at this time or when you are engrossed in some mental activity, that the mental layer will be bright yellowish colour.

Think of the mental layer as your vehicle of perception and awareness and know that this is where your memory, creativity and imagination begins and be consciously aware that every thought that you think carries with it a vibration that will in fact be mirrored back to you.

MENTAL PEACE EXERCISE

This exercise will help you to enjoy mind drifting and the activation of mental peace within the mental layer. You will only need 10 minutes a day to practice these exercises that will help you to "quieten" your mind, helping your body become more relaxed, and in the flow of life.

Mind drifting means that you aware of how you are feeling right now, in the present moment. You will bring your mental layer back into equilibrium by using this exercise.

If you can make an audio recording of the following exercise you will feel the positive effect quite quickly. You are probably thinking that you do not wish to listen to your own voice because you feel embarrassed, do not be.

Recording your own script means that you have the power to adjust your rhythm, volume, tone and pitch to one where you would feel comfortable with while listening back to it!

Find somewhere quiet. Turn off all of the phones and ask not to be disturbed for 20 minutes. (Sometimes families or spouses take umbrage to you having some 'you time', however ask them to support you by giving you just 20 minutes)

Make your space warm and comfortable, light a candle and perhaps some lavender oil or some incense.

It is best to sit up as you may fall asleep if you lie down.

Mental Peace Exercise...

Sit up straight, either in a chair or on the floor.
(You can also try a cross-legged position if you wish)
If you are sitting up then sit barefoot
with you feet on the floor.
If any distracting thoughts or images that come into your mind
do not pay them any attention.
Simply release them in a yellow bubble.

Close your eyes and let your eyelids become heavy.

Keeping your eyes closed raise your eyeballs
just above the lids and remain like this.

Let your shoulders drop and become heavy.
Release the tension in your jaw, allow it to fall open.
Allow your tongue to relax and become heavy.

Breathe in for a count of 4, breathing in the
universal life force energy, drift, drift and drifting.

Hold for the count of 4, feeling the wonderful energy
fill your entire being.

Exhale for the count of 4, feel as you breathe out
you are releasing all mental activity.

Imagine that you have an oversized pair of shoes on your feet that have hundreds of roots that travel into Mother Earth.

Repeat by breathing in for a count of 4, breathing in the universal white light energy, drift, drift and drifting.

Hold for a count of 4, feel the wonderful white light energy encompassing your mind, body and spirit.

Exhale for a count of 4; feel as you breathe out you are releasing all mental chatter.

Now imagine that you can mentally push the roots down into the earth's core.
Stay with this deep, relaxing, peaceful feeling of bliss.

Feel the subtle energy vibrations running up from Mother Earth through the roots to the feet...calves and shins...thighs... to the base of the spine...moving up the spine to the stomach... up the spine past the chest to the throat and now allow the energy vibrations to move out of the crown of your head like a fountain.

Become aware of the warmth and tingling above your head. Feel the white light energy vibrations running down in the crown...still running down the spine...to the throat...chest... stomach...base of the spine...into the thighs...calves and shins... feet...into the roots. You are now grounded.

Begin to sense and feel the energy extending right out into infinity.

Sense the energy now very clearly above your head.

Allow the white light energy to drench all of the layers.

Now feel the energy to channel down into your crown. Allow it to fill your entire being.

Keep breathing in for a count of 4, holding for a count of 4 and then releasing for a count of 4.

Feel the warming energy flooding and filling your mental layer, healing and expanding through the mental layer, removing negative unproductive thought patterns.

Feel your connection to the universal energy and light, and know that you are at one with yourself.

THE ASTRAL BODY - 4TH LAYER

The Astral Layer or fourth layer is the first spiritual layer and is the interaction of the physical and spiritual planes. It is the connection of the physical lower three layers to the upper three layers.

The astral layer is the portal to the astral plane where all energy must pass through when moving from the physical world to the spiritual world. If any imbalances are present in any of the layers, it will have an influence on the other layers causing further imbalances.

It is through the astral layer that you are united with love and where the healing energy comes from. The astral layers colours are very similar to the emotional layer, except it is pervaded with the colour rose pink which is connected to the heart chakra.

Have you ever heard people say after a relationship or friendship has ended "I feel torn in two" or "I feel torn apart" or "I feel that my heart has been ripped out"? This is because any form of interaction is an energy interaction and when a relationship or friendship is formed, cords from our chakras exchange, and energy and information are exchanged along these cords and connections.

The stronger the relationship or bond is then the stronger the emotional interaction will be whether positive or negative. It is through these cords that we are bound together with another person, and the stronger the connection is whether positive or negative, will have a huge impact on the relationship.

I am a Reiki Master Teacher and I know that without a shadow of a doubt that severed cords can be repaired and healed, it is a gradual process of course, as all healing is.

Vibrational healing is an amazing model for various kinds of healing. Vibrational healing is nothing new it has been practiced for thousands of years, and is now being used in hospitals complementing allopathic medicine.

Aura Cleansing Exercise...

Close your eyes and take in three breaths through the nose.

Hold for the count of 3 and release slowly.

Stand with your feet 12" apart and your hands by your side.

Close your eyes and continue breathing in for the count of 3, holding and slowly releasing on the count of 3.

You are standing under a beautiful waterfall.
You can feel the water pouring down over your head...
shoulders, chest and back...all the way down over your feet.

It moves over your entire being, cascading down into the earth.

Let the water cleanse your energy layers deeply, and on every level.

Let your unwanted energy be washed down into Mother Earth.

As your unwanted energy is being washed away say 3 times
"I release all negativity from my mind,.my body and my aura"

You will feel a sense of release flowing all around and within you.

When you are ready open your eyes...stretch your arms above
your head...move your feet around...you now feel clean and refreshed

If you would like to learn more about the layers within your aura; there is a further three layers which are 'The Etheric Template' 'The Celestial Body' and 'The Ketheric Template'. The etheric template layer forms a template for the etheric energy body and it is in this layer where sound creates matter.

The celestial layer is the emotional level of the spiritual plane; it is in this layer that we discover unconditional love. The Ketheric template is the outer layer that encompasses the energy layers complete with the chakras.

TIPS ON YOUR ENERGY FIELD AND AURA

Everything is energy.

All of your thoughts, feelings, words, deeds and actions,
are all flows of energy patterns.

Your energy field (otherwise known as Aura, Prana, Chi or Life Force
Energy) is constantly flowing and interacting with the physical world.

Your energy field is continuously absorbing and processing
the energies of the atmosphere, people and places.

Moment-by-moment your energy field is constantly flowing
with incoming and outgoing energy material which
has to be processed and then stored.

What isn't processed is stored as memories, interactions,
distress and trauma, disease from the past. All of which are negative

Certain emotions and thought patterns can become stuck
within the energy field, if this happens long after the experience
has ended; it is because the 'energy connection' remains intact.
If this was a distressing experience, then the effects
you will be feeling will not be serving you –
resulting in fatigue and an emotionally 'drained' feeling.

Stagnant energy can in fact prevent you from moving forward in your life.

By clearing un-productive energies from your energy field,
you will discharge any blockages or stagnation
thereby allowing unrestricted energy to move freely,
bringing about balance to you entire being.

> **The body never lies**
> Martha Graham

CONCLUSION TO THE ENERGY LAYERS

So you can see from the above that to maintain a strong and healthy life force, energy is extremely important. When the life force energy becomes congested or stagnant physical disease and ill health will manifest within the body. To embrace good health and well-being our life force energy needs to be free flowing in a clear and balanced way.

Where there are unwanted and unproductive patterns present that do not serve you well, it is possible to heal and transform these through 'The Universal Garden Series'.

CHAPTER 13
CHAKRAS

This section on chakras offers deeper ways of looking at your physical health and well being on all levels. Previously we talked about the auric layer offering insight into how emotional dis-harmony can be the originator of illness, which then shows how dis-harmony within the auric layers often represents a message.

Dis-ease of the body and sickness is often the last resort; it is a cry for help from your true self for you to release outdated thinking and behavioural patterns; which in turn will implement change for you to follow your true path in life.

Chakras are non-physical energy centres that are vortices of energy that spin, distributing energy to flow from one chakra to another. Chakras become energy funnels for the energy to flow in and out of your aura.

The chakras are constantly exchanging energy from one level to another to the physical body through the endocrine system that regulates other systems in the body. The chakra function is to vitalise the physical body and bring about development of your self-awareness.

Chakras are associated with your physical, mental and emotional interactions.

Knowledge is the antidote to fear.
Ralph Waldo Emerson

When the chakra energy is unobstructed and flowing freely, the energy will be balanced and you will experience a sense of physical well-being.

Whilst your physical body is enjoying good health and well being, your mind will be enjoying peace of mind.

Free flowing energy brings about equilibrium to the chakras, therefore mental clarity is achieved.

Everything is energy

and you offer vibrations with your thoughts, words, feelings, deeds and actions.

When your chakras are balanced and energy is flowing freely, you are vibrating at a higher frequency, permitting you to enjoy your true connection to the universal energies. If your chakras are deficient or in excess, obstructions will be present and therefore there are problems in your day-to-day living and well being.

There are many chakras; however we will be concentrating on the main seven.

The seven main chakras are located between the top of the head and the base of the spine and are linked with the spinal column in an upward flow of energy and are the areas where major energy flows intersect.

Now let's look at The 7 Chakras in more depth as they affect everyone and everything in our lives.

Each independent chakra is related to a specific sound, colour, subtle layer, gemstone, gland, sense, angel, musical note, tone and function.

Chakra	Sound	Colour	Subtle Layer	Gemstone	Function	Gland	Sense	Angel
1 Base/Root	Lam	Red	Etheric	Ruby or Garnet	Action	Adrenal	Smell	Chamuel
2 Sacral	Vam	Orange	Emotional	Carnelian	Emotion	Reproductive Organs	Taste	Uriel
3 Solar Plexus	Ram	Yellow	Mental	Citrine	Power	Pancreas	Eyesight	Raphael
4 Heart	Yam	Green or Pink	Astral	Rose Quartz	Compassion	Thymus	Touch	Gabriel
5 Throat	Ham	Blue	Etheric	Sodalite	Communication	Thyroid	Hearing	Zadkiel
6 Third Eye	Ksham	Indigo	Celestial	Lapis Lazuli	Vision	Pituitary	Vision	Ariel
7 Crown	Om	Violet or White	Ketheric	Amethyst or White Topaz	Fulfilment	Pineal	Empathy	Metatron

1. THE BASE OR ROOT CHAKRA

The Base Chakra is located at the base of the spine.

The colour association is red.

It is this chakra that keeps you grounded and living.

It is connected with the etheric layer of the aura.

It is also linked to physical sensation.

Imagine children's building blocks, now imagine the building blocks are your seven chakras, if the first or one of the bricks isn't balanced correctly the whole set of bricks will fall, the chakras are no different. If your base chakra is out of balance and suffering restricted energy flow it will not be eliminating toxic energy, resulting in your entire energy system encountering a build up of toxic energy. It is important to exercise the chakras regularly for the root chakra to keep your energy system running at optimum performance.

When this chakra is not firing on all cylinders the lack of wealth and abundance is prevalent. People hoard money. They have a fear of losing what they already have and think this is their lot in life, therefore obstructing the ability to receive.

When the root chakra is flowing freely there is the belief that there is enough to go around for everyone. 'The Universal Garden of Angels' is an excellent place to be for chakra cleansing, as you can ask the angels for assistance regarding this and they will certainly assist you in the clearing process, leaving you feeling more in the flow of life.

The majority of people will have root chakra disparity, this is because most people are not grounded and do not have true belief in themselves and what they represent in this world. If the base chakra is not functioning correctly it will not be eliminating toxic energy, therefore your whole energy system will malfunction.

I have included a grounding exercise at the end of this chapter, for you to use every morning; I suggest that you ground yourself whist taking a shower as it is a nice gentle way to start the day.

BALANCED AND FLOWING

When the base chakra is balanced and in flow you will feel grounded and secure, enjoying positive physical energy and abundance, living and loving life to the full. A balanced base chakra offers a sense of inner security, good well-being and a strong sense of presence.

ENERGY IN EXCESS

When the base chakra is in excess it draws together large amounts of energy and therefore has difficulty in moving the energy either downwards to the ground, or up to the other parts of the body, this is due to rigidity. Because of the solidness in the area of the base chakra you will struggle to embrace change. Trust will also be an issue when the base chakra energy is in excess, you will also experience fear of survival, food overeating leading to obesity, rigid boundaries, hoarding, being judgemental, boredom, stiffness, sluggishness, greed and material obsession. You will probably have a feeling of being stuck in life, unable to get your feet off the ground; if this is the case for you, then you will find that reading 'The Universal Garden of Releasing and Letting Go' is especially recommended, as it allows for the releasing of outdated beliefs, releasing negative energy within and helping to lose the rigidity within your base chakra.

ENERGY DEFICIENCY

When the base chakra energy is deficient you will be experiencing insecurities and a lack of self confidence, feeling unloved and unlovable with your sex drive very low. Your thought processing will be rigid, you feel unworthy, misunderstood and unhappy.

The reason for you being at such a low ebb is the deficiency in the base chakra is so constricted that any energy moving internally is redirected and distributed aimlessly all the way through the body, the grounding exercise we spoke about earlier is excellent for rebalancing your energy hence keeping you grounded which will in turn bring about a general sense of well being.

The root chakra is associated with the adrenal glands, which spring into action when our survival is threatened and which govern the fight or flight response when we are in danger. It is associated with the first auric layer, the etheric body, which is bluish gray in colour and extends to about one inch from the physical body following all its contours both internally and externally.

2. THE SACRAL CHAKRA

The Sacral Chakra is located between
the base chakra and your navel
(it is about 2-3 inches below your navel).

The colour association is orange.
❈
It is this chakra that is connected
to the reproductive organs.
❈
It is connected with the emotional layer of the aura.

It is also linked to creativity.

The sacral chakra is located about 2 to 3 inches below the navel, this chakra relates to your energy distribution, kidney functions, prostate, ovaries and testicles, sexuality and reproduction.

It controls relationships and your interactions with people in your life. When the sacral chakra is functioning correctly, you have a high level of sexual sensual energy, if there is obstruction present, your sex drive will be weak.

The sacral chakra is your creativity centre.

This chakra is related with the emotional level and your mysterious powers of intuition and psychic abilities are awakened when flowing correctly. It is your power centre for inspiration.

Unprocessed emotions will cause energetic obstructions in this chakra, therefore by processing and feeling the emotions, you can release them and let them go, allowing the energy to flow freely.

BALANCED AND FLOWING

When your sacral chakra is balanced and flowing, you are grounded and feel safe, secure and nurtured. You will be at one with yourself and feel powerful. You express your emotions in a dignified manner and have them under control. You will love and feel comfortable being intimate and passionate, being at one with your sexuality.

ENERGY IN EXCESS

Emotionally explosive, overly ambitious, manipulative, caught up in illusions, overindulgent, having high sexual energy, often seeing people as only sex objects.

When this chakra is out of balance, issues regarding self respect, fear of losing control, financial loss, ability to survive and thrive, poorly balanced relationships will be present. Eating issues such as anorexia and bulimia, along with buried emotions and depression are associated with an unbalanced second chakra.

ENERGY DEFICIENCY

Shy, timid, immobilized by fear, overly sensitive, self negating, burdened by guilt, sexual energy-clinging, guilty about having sex, abused, frigid or impotent.

A CLIENT'S STORY

A client who originally came to see me in 2005 for life coaching benefited enormously from chakra balancing.

Usually when new clients come to see me they generally feel apprehensive and understandably a little nervous at their first appointment. But, this client was overly tense, she appeared to be taut, nervy emotionally and she seemed stiff as she walked, her attitude seemed quite detached too. I instinctively knew that her energy was severely depleted in several of the chakras; however after checking her chakra energy the most prominent one was the sacral chakra.

As she relaxed into the session she told me that she was 29 years old and an only child; both her parents had very rigid viewpoints about many things; however the main one was that sex was a dirty act; my client therefore was ingrained with this belief.

She still lived at home with her parents and worked full time as a civil servant, and had no social life. Several of the girls at work asked her out to the cinema or to the pub quiz; however she never had the courage to meet up with them, it was as if she thought that she wasn't meant to have fun.

She told me that she had never experienced a relationship with a man let alone a sexual encounter in her life. Through being trapped in her love less and sexless life she felt extremely isolated, encountering low self-esteem and self-confidence. She was also very confused, lethargic and very sad. Her belief system was in pieces. Beliefs are about how we think things really are, what we think is really true and what therefore we expect as likely consequences that will follow from our behaviour.

Initially we worked in 'The Universal Garden of Love' as I knew that this client had no self love at all, in fact I would say that when it came to love she was devoid of it, she was numb. Before you can move on in life you have to discover love within you.

We also worked with colour to balance her chakra. As foods carry a colour vibration, she ate lots of orange coloured foods, peppers, mangos, butternut squash, carrots and of course oranges.

Although she was initially uncomfortable to wear orange clothes she was very brave and starting wearing not only orange in her clothing but in her accessories as well.

She carried with her everyday and everywhere, a piece of raw carnelian gemstone (orange in colour); it was to her like a security blanket. After about six weeks she seemed more confident and more at ease and more comfortable in her own skin so I suggested that maybe with her new found confidence she should try a part time evening job, which hopefully would lead to her finally starting a social life.

A couple of weeks later she managed to get a part time job working behind the bar in the club house of a local rugby club. She fitted in really well and as the people at the club had no preconceived ideas about her they accepted her as she was, a funny attractive woman, she discovered that she loved to laugh and have fun.

The job at the rugby club did not feel like a job to her she loved being there so much, even more so when she met Gareth who played rugby at the club.

Gareth asked her out and things very quickly gathered pace with her discovering true love with him. They now have Jack their little one year old who keeps them on their toes. Her parents unfortunately have not forgiven her for the change in her life; however the great thing is she has forgiven them.

This story shows how powerfully both positively and negatively your chakras rule your body and life; if you pay attention to your chakras you will take control of your life in a positive way.

3. THE SOLAR PLEXUS CHAKRA

✧

The Solar Plexus Chakra is located
about 4" above the navel.

✧

The colour association is yellow.

✧

It is this chakra that is your power house.

✧

It is connected with the mental layer of the aura.

✧

It is also linked to personal power.

The solar plexus is located about three to four inches above the navel and the best way to discover this chakra is by placing your dominant hand there, the sensations will feel warm and right.

Now rub the palm of your hand in a clockwise circular movements for about two or three minutes and indentify how great this feels and when you stop simply hold it there for thirty seconds and as you pull away be aware of the energy between your tummy and your hand, it feels tingly and possibly stretchy. This is you manipulating your own personal energy.

The colour associated with this chakra is the colour yellow. It is this area where our soul sleeps and defines your "sense of worth". It is here where the ego is formed. This chakra is your power house, it is the seat of your emotion and it is here that you feel by way of your gut instinct.

When we decide that we wish for something we firstly see it through our imagination (the third eye chakra) and then we have to create it by taking action to bring it to you (the sacral chakra). Then the most significant part of the process is to feel it in your solar plexus and it is only then will your desires begin to manifest.

BALANCED AND FLOWING

When the solar plexus is balanced and flowing correctly you can face up to anything as the world is your oyster. You have great control over your life, radiate personality and are happy with a wonderful sense of humour, good will and feel powerful. You are responsible, reliable with self discipline and able to deal with all challenges in a positive way.

ENERGY IN EXCESS

When the solar plexus energy is in excess it will be lacking in power and energy and have feelings of abandonment, helplessness and trying to control not just themselves also others too. They will more than likely be rigid in will and end up with either a temper tantrum or retreating with fear. To overcome those feelings they can become obsessive and controlling, always active and doing, never ceasing.

ENERGY DEFICIENCY

When the solar plexus energy is deficient there is 'no fire in the belly' the energy is low and sluggish and self esteem has retreated to non existence. There may be tummy trouble in the upper digestive tract and constantly feel as if the tummy is in knots. Blame and criticism will definitely make themselves at home. Constant activity is also present and the victim mentality will also make itself known.

4. THE HEART CHAKRA

✸
The Heart Chakra is located between the breasts.
✸
The colour association is green or pink.
✸
It is this chakra that is connected to unconditional love, feeling compassion, empathy, forgiveness, acceptance, peace and harmony.
✸
It is connected with the astral layer of the aura.
✸
It is also linked giving and receiving love.

The Heart Chakra is the centre that exudes love. It is vital that you understand what your needs are for you to attain true love in your life.

The heart chakra is also linked to the joy and happiness in our hearts and the love we feel for ourselves.

This chakra demands self love, respect and compassion; if you do not possess any of these qualities and do not accept yourself then love, peace and harmony will elude you.

Balance your mind, body, and spirit with the golden thread of love in your heart and spiritual food for your spiritual growth.

BALANCED AND FLOWING

When the heart chakra is balanced and flowing you take in the world around you in a positive and healthy way, reaching out to those you are happy being around, giving and receiving love. Compassion is the key to this chakra being balanced and flowing; reverence, truthfulness and self respect will be forerunners in your day-to-day life. A balanced heart chakra offers emotional healing and self acceptance.

ENERGY IN EXCESS

When the heart chakra is in excess we literally become excessive in our relationships and emotions, leading to you becoming a drama queen with over dramatisations and in some cases very manipulative. You need constant assurance and jealousy will be prominent; you will have feelings of addictions to love.

ENERGY DEFICIENCY

When the heart chakra energy is deficient you will be reactive to certain experiences which lead to you reacting by withdrawing from society. You may also be experiencing visiting past relationships in your mind where you were loved but where the relationship is now ceased. You may become withdrawn, insensitive and critical; when this happens there is a need for you to forgive yourself and learn to have acceptance of you. It is essential that you learn to love yourself again.

Your heart chakra is not only a vital organ but the balance between the upper and the lower chakras, for it to become healed, balanced and strong you need to discover the golden thread of love.

5. THE THROAT CHAKRA

✦
The Throat Chakra is located at the throat.
✦
The colour association is powder blue.
✦
It is this chakra that is connected to exclaiming your truth and voicing your opinion.
✦
It is connected with the etheric template layer of the aura.
✦
It is also linked to truthfulness and service.

The throat chakra is the centre from where we speak our truth.

It relates to your expression of communication, speech and capacity to communicate.

Reciting poetry, chanting an affirmation or singing is a must for the throat chakra.

Listening is also a great thing as this pleases those around you and also stops the inner chatter of your mind.

BALANCED AND FLOWING

When the throat chakra is balanced and flowing freely you are able to focus well, listen to what is going on around you and be compassionate to those in your life. You will come across as enigmatic and a top notch communicator with energy that flows in a positive way. You are able to take the lead role directing those around you with care and compassion, communicating in a powerful way and with confidence and self belief.

ENERGY IN EXCESS

When the throat chakra is in excess you will find you talk gobbled-de-gook by talking far too much or gossiping about others. You will also be annoying to others due to your inability to listen to what people have to say by not grasping what they mean; constantly interrupting people when they are speaking and always trying to control the conversation.

ENERGY DEFICIENCY

When the Throat chakra is deficient you simply cannot get the words out of your mouth and you will have a fear of speaking up for yourself. You will have problems putting how you feel into words and struggle with feelings of embarrassment and introversion.

6. THE THIRD EYE CHAKRA

The Third Eye Chakra is located
between the eyebrows.

The colour association is indigo blue.

It is this chakra that is connected to spiritual vision.

It is connected with the celestial body layer
of the aura.

It is also linked to meditation and visualisation.

The third eye chakra is a dark indigo blue colour.

Your third eye is what you use to visualise whatever you wish to manifest.

It is here that you see it first. You know the old saying "I will believe it when I see it" this is not so, you have to "see it and believe it!" for it to manifest.

The third eye is your spiritual eye and your psychic awareness is developed here, therefore any negative thoughts and fears regarding your spiritual beliefs will definitely obstruct the energy flow here.

The third eye chakra is the ability to think straight, as well as your sense of imagination, intuition, wisdom, and consciousness.

BALANCED AND FLOWING

When the third eye chakra is balanced and flowing freely you are endowed with the gift of being intuitive and your perceptions are excellent. You will also discover that your visualisation techniques are enhanced with the power of recalling your memories quite easily. You are able to focus well, listen to what is going on around you and be compassionate to those in your life.

ENERGY IN EXCESS

When the third eye chakra is in excess you will find yourself feeling under the weather and you may possibly experience the inability to place your focus and concentrate on certain things. The third eye chakra also relates to problems such as hallucinations and nightmares both of which can lead to relentless headaches and eye problems.

ENERGY DEFICIENCY

When the third eye chakra is deficient you simply cannot see the wood for the trees, this leaves you unable to think correctly or have any imagination; leaving you unable to do what the third eye does best and that is to envision your desires through visualisation.

7. THE CROWN CHAKRA

The Crown Chakra is located
at the crown of the head.

The colour association is purple.

This chakra that is connected
to spiritual healing energy.

It is connected with the Ketheric body layer
of the aura.

It is also linked to mind, body and spirit matters.

The crown chakra is at your crown. The crown chakra is the last of the seven major chakras and the colour associated with it is violet through to white. The relationship of the crown chakra is in association with knowledge, deep inner wisdom, deep perception and a connection to the divine offering of a higher state of enlightenment and spiritual growth.

Your life force energy flows into your crown chakra down through all of the other chakras to the base chakra and back again. Each chakra needs to be unobstructed in order for the energy to be free flowing. To ensure that your crown chakra is unobstructed open yourself up and tap in to the divine powers of the universe with deep belief and above all TRUST.

When negativity has made itself at home you may possibly be fearful of any form of spirituality or religion, this fear or disbelief will definitely obstruct the flowing of energies in the crown chakra.

There is nothing outside of yourself to be fearful of; it is only you that allows the fear in. You can be spiritual and not believe in any religion at all. The crown chakra signifies unification with the higher self, the universe, and the divine.

Attachment is also associated with the crown chakra; attachment to things of the material world is the key to this chakra being out of balance.

If you are feeling materialistic, release all attachment and let go of any need to control what you may have and release addictive habits that formed because of how you perceive the world through your belief system.

When you release and let go of all attachment you will experience the world in a completely different way and discover the splendour of who you truly are.

Willpower is the key to success.
Successful people strive no matter what they feel
by applying their will to overcome apathy, doubt or fear.
Dan Millman

BALANCED AND FLOWING

When the crown chakra is balanced and flowing freely you are able to release all attachments to all areas of your life.

The crown chakra is the highest vibrating chakra and when unobstructed and free flowing gives access to unlimited divine inspiration.

When all of the other chakras are free flowing too, you are an expression to manifest, express, and live a life that is truly amazing.

ENERGY IN EXCESS

Symptoms of excessive energy in the crown chakra mean we tend to hideaway not wishing to face up to the things in our lives. We have feelings of loneliness that leave us feeling disconnected from the world around us.

We encounter strong feelings of doubt about ourselves and our world around us.

ENERGY DEFICIENCY

Deficiency in the crown chakra results in feelings of detachment, rigid belief systems, and a restricted and congested mind.

You will experience fear of spirituality and a lack of purpose in life. Taking in new things maybe difficult as the learning process is affected. Life feels stagnant and pointless.

You may have intense feelings of low self-esteem and self-denial. You could feel misunderstood. You cannot see the bigger picture in life.

A GROUNDING EXERCISE

Your physical body is your vessel through this life and it is important to take care and protect your vessel.
Protection is done through grounding yourself on a daily basis through visualisation exercises.

Grounding exercises are an excellent way of keeping yourself grounded, stopping you from becoming flighty, helping you connect to mother earth through your base chakra.

For the exercise...

Go into a quiet place, where you will not be disturbed.

If you have a partner or a family let them know that you are going to have a little quiet time for you and ask that you are not to be disturbed.

I love this part of this exercise, I teach it to my students in Reiki.
Now place one hand on your chest and the other one on your stomach, it does not matter which hand is on the stomach or which is on the chest.

For the breathing part of this exercise it is better to breathe in through your nose and out through your mouth, however please breathe how you feel is the most comfortable for you.

Practice this as many times as you wish.

This exercise should be repeated each morning; as you get used to the process, you will find you gain more and more benefit, there is no better way to start each day than with this amazing grounding technique.

Grounding Exercise...

Now, take a slow deep breath in through your nose to the count of 1...2...3...4
Hold this breath in for the count of 1...2...3...4

Breathe out through your mouth to the count of or 1...2...3...4 releasing any tension, concerns and anxieties as you exhale.

You will discover as you inhale that the hand on your chest will hardly move at all but the hand on your stomach will rise.
When you exhale the hand on your stomach will move inwards.

Take a slow deep breath in through your nose to the count of 1...2...3...4
Hold this breath in for the count of 1...2...3...4

Breathe out through your mouth to the count of 1...2...3...4
The more oxygen that you take in, the less tense and anxious you will feel. (You can perform this breathing technique anytime that you wish, so whenever you feel stressed, slow down and breathe deeply).

Now I am going to ask you to imagine that you have a pair of oversized soft suede shoes on your feet...
Now imagine that your very soft suede shoes have hundreds of roots on the base of each shoe...

Imagine the roots are growing and pushing down into Mother Earth...
Feel the roots moving and feel the tingling in your feet and ankles...

Now imagine that you have a silver cord that runs from the base of your spine through your feet into the ground, pushing down into Mother Earth...
Feel the silver cord pushing down, deeper and deeper into Mother Earth...
Now feel the tingle at the base of the spine...

Begin to bring the energy of Mother Earth up through the silver cord and hold the energy at the base of the spine...

Keeping your breathing steady and even...Begin to bring the energy of Mother Earth up through the roots on the shoes...to your feet......calves and shins... to the base of your spine and hold it there... feeling the tingling...
Keeping your breathing steady and even...

Now continue to keep all of the energy at the base of the spine...Begin to move all of the Mother Earth Energy up past your navel...Moving up until you reach your breast bone...Moving it to your throat area...
Moving it between the eyebrows...Keeping your breathing steady and even...Imagine that your crown can open...

Allow all of the Mother Earth energy to shoot out of your crown...
Imagine a fountain showering you with wonderful Mother Earth energy...

Keeping your breathing steady and even...Your crown is still fully open...
Imagine about ten inches above your crown there is a pale blue cosmic light beaming down...

Allow the pale blue cosmic light to beam down into your crown...to your third eye...throat...heart centre...solar plexus...sacral...base chakra...
You are now connected to Mother Earth and the Universal energies.

When you are ready open your eyes.
Take a little sip of still water and feel yourself coming back slowly and gently.

PART TWO
THE GARDENS

In Part Two of the Universal Gardens Pathfinder you will discover the Universal Garden Wheel which will help you choose which Gardens can help you in your journey through life.

You will then learn about each of twelve Universal Gardens, what lies within them and how they can help you change your world.

Part Two will give you an exciting taste of the unique possibilities that await you in the Universal Gardens!

You can visit each garden and use your time there to dramatically break your old habits and develop a new way of thinking. You can change your life by using the powerful techniques you have seen in **Part One** and combining them with time spent in the garden of your choice.

THE UNIVERSAL GARDEN WHEEL

The Universal Garden Wheel is the technique I use to discover which Garden will be the most advantageous for my clients at a particular time in their lives.

By using this method you will identify which areas of your life require focus and nurturing and therefore which of The Universal Gardens will be of most benefit.

Within the wheel there are 12 gardens, you simply mark your score out of 10 relating to where you feel you are at this moment in time relating to that garden.

The higher the score the more fulfilment you have in that part of your life, the lower the score relates to the amount of discontentment you have.

Let's look at some examples so you can clearly see how to do this.

If you need copies of the Universal Garden Wheel,
go to the 'Downloads' area at www.TheUniversalGardens.com.

We have provided blank wheels for you to download and use.

> There is deep wisdom within our very flesh,
> if we can only come to our senses and feel it.
> Elizabeth A. Behnke

EXAMPLE OF ONE PERSON'S GARDEN WHEEL

This person's score is summarised in the table below.

First they scored between 0 and 10 for each of the 12 gardens.

This can then be transferred onto a blank wheel, to graphically show the scores on the Garden Wheel.

Their Garden Wheel is shown opposite.

Garden	Score
Money	2
Love	5
Healing	1
Forgiveness	0
Releasing and Letting Go	0
Gratitude	4
Dreams and Aspirations	2
Goals and Desires	2
Angels	5
Guardian Angel	4
Crystal Healing	5
Fountain of Youth	0

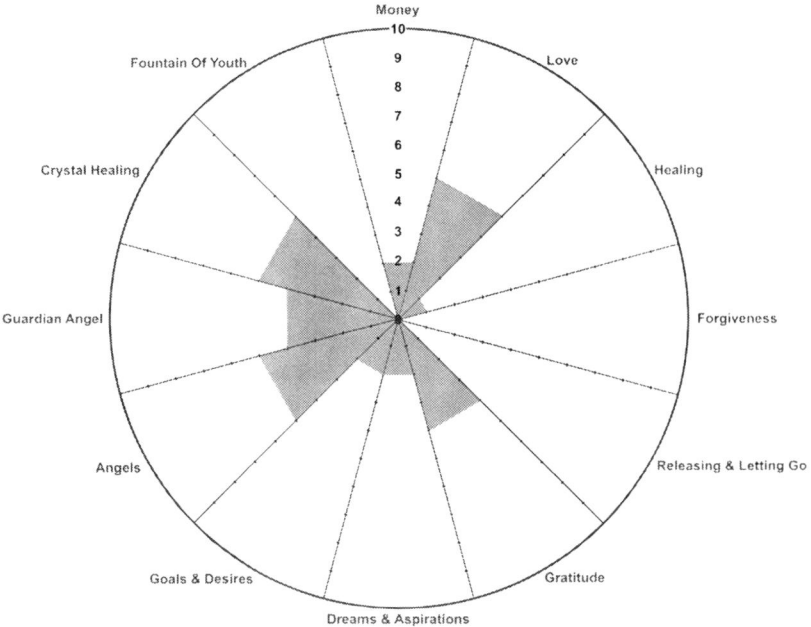

THIS PERSON'S GARDEN WHEEL RESULTS IN THE FOLLOWING ANALYSIS...

Money = 2

With a score of 2 this person is in a poor financial situation; this may be from a lack of money or this person is overspending greatly. The Money Garden is for this person, it will help them to change their poor financial situation resulting in stress and unhappiness, in to one of abundance and financial freedom.

Love = 5

With a score of 5 this persons relationships are neither great nor poor. They might have satisfactory love from their partner, friends or family but it is not great. To discover the golden thread of love at a truly great level visiting 'The Love Garden' will attract love to their very core whether it be from their partner, family or friends.

Healing = 1

With a score of 1 this person's health and well being is very poor and is in great need of urgent attention. In times like this, 'The Healing Garden' is the place to go to create the healthy, happy life you desire with greater ease.

Forgiveness = 0

With a score of 0 this person cannot forgive anything or anybody for what is probably a challenging life. Forgiveness is the key to leading a healthy happy life; being unforgiving restricts all aspects of your life. When you forgive and let go of negative judgments you release the shackles of the ball and chain that restricts you and holds you back. Visiting 'The Forgiveness Garden' will invite this person into a whole new world where forgiveness results in a happy, healthy and contended life.

Releasing and letting go = 0

With a score of 0 this person cannot and will not let go of negative issues, either present or from the past. Releasing and letting go of your past means you are releasing attachment to your negative memories. Visiting 'The Releasing and Letting Go Garden' will help you find the golden key of happiness by allowing the flood gates to open for more wonderful things to come into your life.

Gratitude = 4

With a score of 4 this person has gratitude for things in their life but it is less than average. Gratitude is an attitude, the more gratitude you have for the things you have in your life; the more you will receive things to be grateful for. Visiting 'The Gratitude Garden' will enter you into the state of gratefulness every day and discover your golden thread of love flowing from your heart. The Garden allows gratitude to be at the forefront of everything and everyone in your life.

Dreams and Aspirations = 2

With a score of 2 this person is suffering from poor dreams and aspirations. For your dreams and aspirations to become reality visiting 'The Dreams and Aspirations Garden' will help you to bring your dreams and aspirations into fruition.

Goals and Desires = 2

With a score of 2 this person has very few goals and desires. We all should have goals and desires, whether it is for a new car, job promotion or even wanting to make new friends. The 'Goals and Desires Garden' will help you to not only set the goals and desires you seek; but show you how to achieve them. 'The Goals and Desires Garden' coaches you to understand that your dominant thoughts are what you become and how important goal setting is. Goal setting is essential in achieving success because it keeps you focused on what is really important to you.

Angels = 5

This person has a score of 5 so they are at least half way towards being at one with the beautiful divine angels. Going into The Angel Garden will enhance your entire being, offering to you meaningful purpose that you can embrace. The Angel Garden will help you to identify the sculptor within you for you to sculpt the life of your dreams. The Angels will help you to live the life you love and love the life you live.

Guardian Angel = 4

This person has a score of 4 so may believe that they have a Guardian Angel but do not know of the benefits their Guardian Angel can offer from their birth till their death. By visiting 'The Guardian Angel Garden' you will learn how to identify your Guardian Angel and by working side by side with them you will not only be enhancing the spiritual side of your life but all aspects of your life.

Crystal = 5

This person has a score of 5 so they may realise what potentially crystals can do to change and enhance their lives but do not know how to benefit greatly from their use. Visiting 'The Crystal Garden' you will discover the many ways that crystals enhance all aspects of your life. Discover in 'The Crystal Garden' how to heal and restore balance to your mind body and spirit. The Garden will help you to release and clear negative or obstructive energy, harmonising your mind, body, spirit, and above all else your emotions, enhancing feelings of great well-being.

The Fountain of Youth = 0

This person has a score of 0 indicating that they are not taking care of themselves in either mind, body or spirit what so ever. Stepping into 'The Fountain of Youth Garden' you will discover amazing tools and techniques to hold back father time. The Garden will offer you the techniques to slow down the ageing process, giving you youthfulness as your natural state of mind. You are as young as you think you are and by changing your mind you will change how you look and feel.

He who knows others is learned; he who knows himself is wise.
Lao-tzu, Tao te Ching

The Universal Gardens help you to live every day in every way with interest, exuberant enthusiasm and unending optimism allowing your imagination to run wild beyond your belief.

Grace Brown

USING THE GARDEN WHEEL
A SECOND EXAMPLE

Here is another example of someone using the Garden Wheel.

Again, they have scored themselves between 0 and 10 for each of the 12 gardens.

Opposite, below, you can clearly see how this has transferred onto the Garden Wheel.

Again, to help you, I am going to analyse the results so you can see how each score applies to each garden.

Garden	Score
Money	2
Love	9
Healing	3
Forgiveness	9
Releasing and Letting Go	9
Gratitude	8
Dreams and Aspirations	7
Goals and Desires	7
Angels	2
Guardian Angel	2
Crystal Healing	2
Fountain of Youth	9

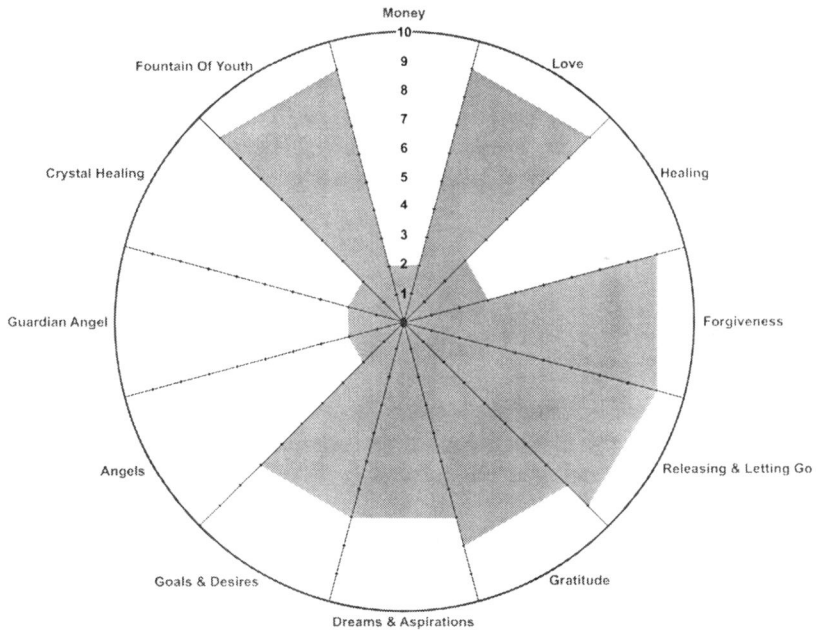

Money = 2

As with the 1st diagram with a score of 2 this person is in a poor financial situation; this may be from a lack of money or this person is overspending greatly.

The Money Garden is for this person, it will help them to change their poor financial situation resulting in stress and unhappiness, in to one of abundance and financial freedom.

Love = 9

With a score of 9, this person is experiencing very high levels of love in their life, they are nearly at their destination of perfect love and unlimited light; they simply have to reach for the stars.

Placing their attention in 'The Love Garden' and becoming focused on love and pure blessedness will help them to achieve perfection.

Healing = 3

With a score of 3 this person's health and well being is quite poor and is in need of attention. Health is a state of mind, 'The Healing Garden' will introduce to them the instinctive qualities this garden possesses which are the very qualities they need to welcome health and well being back into their life.

Forgiveness = 9

With a score of 9 this person is an excellent forgiver, they are not holding on to the past and move through their life with great compassion. They are free, experiencing a blissful and joyful daily life in the area of forgiveness.

If you are finding it hard to forgive people in your past, then to move on in your life to one of pure bliss it is essential that you learn to forgive with 'The Forgiveness Garden'.

Releasing and Letting Go = 9

With a score of 9 this person is completely happy to let things go, which is excellent. They have programmed themselves to release and let go all negativities from their past. Releasing and letting go is a discipline and this person deals with adversity head on. If you are struggling to release the negative things that have happened to you in the past then 'The releasing and Letting Go' garden will guide you to begin this important process.

Gratitude = 8

With a score of 8 this person has gratitude in abundance in their life. Scoring 8 on the wheel for Gratitude they are enjoying a state of gratefulness every day with their golden thread of love flowing through them. They are happy and grateful for the people in their life; they live a lot, laugh a lot and love a lot and continue on their gratitude journey.

Visiting 'The Gratitude Garden' will help them to achieve ultimate love and happiness in their lives. If you are not as fortunate as this person then entering 'The Gratitude Garden' will open up a new world to you, one of love and great happiness.

Dreams and Aspirations 7

With a score of 7 this person can identify with their dreams and aspirations quite well. To achieve ten on the Garden wheel they need to enter the 'Dreams and Aspirations Garden', this garden will help them to not only identify their dreams and aspirations fully but enable them to manifest them into reality.

Remember, whatever you wish for, can and will become yours. You have the golden thread of love running through you and you hold the golden key of your destiny in your subconscious mind. It is all about your belief and trust for it being for your highest good.

Goals and Desires = 7

With a score of 7 again this person can identify and is achieving their goals and desires to a certain degree.

Life is probably quite good for them in most areas, but to take their goals and desires to another plain and on towards perfection they need to continuously go into 'The Goals and Desires Garden' generating that strong desire. Encouraging strong desires results in bringing strong results, whereas weak desires bring weak results.

Angels = 2

With a score of 2 this person does believe that perhaps Angels exist but they certainly do not realise what great power Angels have in helping them to discover what they really want in life; and more importantly helping them achieve what they wish for.

By going into 'The Angel Garden' they will be shown how to discover and travel to the destination that they truly desire to arrive at. It is in 'The Angel Garden' that the door to miracles and magic is opened to you. In 'The Angel Garden' your Angels offer you love and support to grow with the Angels and become who you wish to be.

Guardian Angel = 2

With a score of 2 this person once again may believe that there may or may not be a guardian angel but they certainly do not realise what influence their Guardian Angel has in their life.

Your Guardian Angel Garden enlightens you to your spiritual destiny and the extreme importance in understanding your life path while waiting to feed and nurture you with pure love. Move forward to an ever increasing tapestry of abundance of love and light, prosperity and joy that you are looking to manifest in your life by visiting 'The Guardian Angel Garden'.

Crystal = 2

With a score of 2 this person may think that crystals play some role in life, but they certainly do not realise how crystals can bring balance and harmony within their mind body and spirit. 'The Crystal Garden' works with chakras and the subtle bodies circulating energy to the chakra power points that are essential for balancing and bringing about healing to all aspects of your life. 'The Crystal Garden' opens you up to receiving higher vibrations of energy, connecting you deeply to Source energy, harmonising your entire being.

The Fountain of Youth = 9

With a score of 9 this person is in tip top condition taking extra special care of their own health and well being. Holding back father time is fundamental to looking good and feeling great. By visiting 'The Fountain of Youth Garden' you will find how to cultivate self confidence, self respect and love for you; helping you to deal with whatever life throws at you.

Holding back father time comes from your inner belief about you. Your appearance is of extreme importance because you only have one chance to make a good first impression, you do not get a second chance. Looking and feeling your best gives you confidence, you will find this in 'The Fountain of Youth Garden'.

Self-respect is the fruit of discipline...
Abraham J. Heschel

FILLING IN YOUR PERSONAL UNIVERSAL GARDEN WHEEL

You must fill in your Universal Garden Wheel with complete honesty, the only person you are kidding if you do not is yourself.

So, if you are on the verge of bankruptcy then score the money garden as 1, likewise if you have complete financial freedom then score the money garden as 9. As an assist use the scoring table to help you judge where you are at this particular point of your life.

	Scoring Table	
Number	Scale	Improvements
0	You are not in a great place here - it could not get any worse	Your aim is to raise the bar to 2 or 3
1	Very Poor	Your aim is to raise the bar to 3
2	Poor	Your aim is to raise the bar to 3
3	Quite Poor	Your aim is to raise the bar to 4
4	Below Average	Your aim is to raise the bar to 5
5	Average	Your aim is to raise the bar to 6
6	Higher than average	Your aim is to raise the bar to 7
7	Quite Good	Your aim is to raise the bar to 8
8	Good	Your aim is to raise the bar to 9
9	Very Good	Your aim is to raise the bar to 10
10	What can I say? A perfect Score!	You have to maintain this level

NOW FILL IN YOUR PERSONAL UNIVERSAL GARDEN WHEEL WITH COMPLETE HONESTY.

Garden	Score
Money	
Love	
Healing	
Forgiveness	
Releasing and Letting Go	
Gratitude	
Dreams and Aspirations	
Goals and Desires	
Angels	
Guardian Angel	
Crystal Healing	
Fountain of Youth	

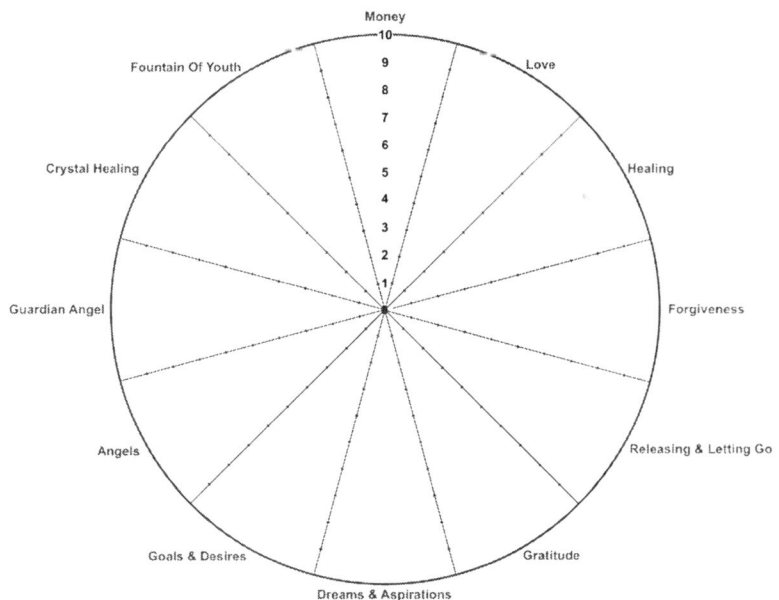

SELECTING YOUR GARDEN

Having filled in each section of your wheel, you should easily see what part of your life needs attention and more importantly which section of your life needs attention now.

The next step is to take action and address the areas that your Universal Garden Wheel has uncovered good or bad. If there is more than one area that needs attention then you should deal with the area with the lowest score first, to gain maximum affect each garden should be worked on for a minimum of at least 30 days.

To change your life takes true commitment. You will be required to go into your chosen Garden at least once a day for a minimum of thirty days and reflect and contemplate last thing in the evening before going to sleep.

Remember that each garden is a journey, and as you improve your life and gain new insights in one area; you must continue working on yourself in other areas of your life and then and only then will the magic happen.

Now you know which garden/s you need to visit, I have listed all 12 gardens in more depth in the following chapters. You will find more information relating to each individual garden which in turn will transform and enhance all aspects of your life.

It is a good idea to be alone in a garden at dawn or dark so that all its shy presence may haunt you and possess you in a reverie of suspended thought.

James Douglas

We are each of us angels with only one wing,
and we can only fly by embracing one another.
Luciano de Crescenzo

THE MONEY GARDEN

Relates to your current financial status,
effectively moving you to a state of financial freedom

Money and women—
They're two of the strongest things in the world.
The things you do for a woman
you wouldn't do for anything else.
Same with money.
Satchel Paige

Energy follows thought.

Thoughts are energy.

The creative process begins
with a single thought.

So whatever your thoughts
are about money
will affect the flow
of money in your life,
positive or negative!

THE MONEY GARDEN

MY FRIEND PHIL'S LOVE OF MONEY

When I was young my friends and I used to love playing out, laughing and generally enjoying our youth. Our little gang of friends totalled ten, one of which was Phil.

Now, Phil had one hobby and past time that he loved dearly, counting money and thinking of ways to gain more money! He had numerous piggy banks and money boxes that were all actually full! He would talk about money with such passion, he liked the feel of it, the smell of it, in fact anything about it.

We would call around to his house and his mum would say "he's not coming out to play he's counting his money"; even when Phil spoke about money you would see such a lustful look in eyes, he loved it! I can even remember him one winter renting his sheepskin coat out to his brothers friends because they were all freezing! He told us all he was going to be a millionaire, forever coming up with money making schemes.

I still see Phil every now and then, he still lives in the area; although usually when I see him he is driving his Rolls Royce to one of the many properties he owns and rents out or one of the many businesses he runs. He is a multi millionaire and a very nice guy who simply loves money and the freedom it gives him; from a young age he always knew what his desire was.

The golden key to success is to know what your desire truly is and once identified to go for it, do not shy away from your desires, embrace them as Phil did and welcome a life full of abundance.

> **Money is not the only answer, but it makes a difference.**
> Barack Obama

How Do You Feel About Money?

Good, not so good, comfortable, not so comfortable? It may be that you do not like to discuss money because you think it is crass or because you are fearful of losing what you have or fearful of never having enough.

Money is simply an energy tool. It is down to how it is or isn't used that establishes its desirable quality. When you make the connection that money is bad and that you are bad for wishing for more, you are on the slippery slope to financial ruin. 'The Universal Money Garden' is an excellent tool for helping you to feel comfortable about money and with this comfort being in a position to create more money than you could ever wish for, while not feeling guilty about it in any way at all.

It is down to your belief system about money where your problem lies, which you are probably unaware of. Your beliefs about money are ingrained within you from a very early age.

Are Your Money Pipes Clogged Up?

Energy follows thought. Thoughts are energy. The creative process begins with a single thought. So whatever your thoughts are about money will affect the flow of money in your life, positive or negative!

Nobody else thinks for you, your thinking is all down to you. How you live your life is down to your past thinking. Your dominant thoughts have emphasised what is prevalent in your life now. It may be prosperity, joy and abundance or it could be fear, worry and lack. You will either be in the flow of abundance or resisting the flow of prosperity in your life.

There is an unlimited supply of money in The Money Garden and in your world; the only reason that you do not have sufficient funds is because you are stopping the flow of it coming to you. Your money pipes are clogged up.

How on earth can you expect to enjoy financial freedom if you have certain beliefs about money? You attract into your life what you are thinking about and what you believe. If you think there is not enough money in this world for everyone you will never have enough money. Giving your attention to something, sets the creative juices flowing, creative energy flows through us and expands, enlivens and charges the object of our attention.

ARE YOU AFRAID OF MONEY?

Either, you have too much or you do not have enough?

The Money Garden will help you to discover if and why you have barriers in your life regarding money. If you allow it, money upsets the dynamics of your life, largely by how you perceive it. It has a huge impact on your health and well being too.

Have you been indoctrinated with?

> You have to work hard for your money!
>
> Money does not grow on trees!
>
> Money is the root of all evil!
>
> Rich people are greedy and tight or bad and evil!

This is what is known as scarcity programming. Many of you will have come from large families where you had to get what you could before your siblings had the rest, others may simply have had a frugal upbringing and were educated to think that there was never enough money to go around and that it was not easily available.

If you have beliefs that there isn't enough to go around then STOP right now, and know and believe that there is ample to go round, enough for everyone! Our universe is a very affluent and abundant place to be and there is plenty of money for everyone.

These are just a few eye openers about how we perceive our beliefs:

> Our beliefs are feelings that we have because of how we perceive things.
>
> Our perceptions create our reality and are therefore powerful.
>
> It is the power of beliefs that creates our lives.

YOU HAVE TO WORK HARD FOR YOUR MONEY?

No you do not, you only think that you have to! As you progress through the Money Garden you will understand that to achieve your dreams and desires you have to feel good, because feeling is the key to attracting. 'You have to work hard for your money' is one of the many statements that have been drummed in to us by family members, teachers, elders, society, peers indeed from all facets and people in our lives.

Why have you been indoctrinated with these statements and beliefs you may wonder, it is how the people that have programmed you have themselves being programmed by others; these beliefs can go back many generations.

What really matters now is that you understand that you really do not have to flog yourself to death to earn money; you only think you have to, and those negative thoughts can be changed. Taking a journey into 'The Money Garden' will show you how to put those negative beliefs in the past and introduce you to new positive abundant beliefs.

> **A thought is merely a thought, and your mere thought can be changed, by changing your mind about it.**
>
> Grace Brown

MONEY DOESN'T GROW ON TREES?

Does money grow on trees? Yes, of course it does in a way, as the higher denomination of money is printed on paper and paper comes from trees. It all comes down to our society's beliefs, and foggy misconceptions.

When you feel these negative or positive beliefs at the core of your being, do these feelings make you feel good or bad? Do these feelings light a fire in your belly or put the fire in your belly out? If it isn't making you feel good, then I strongly believe that working through 'The Money Garden' will completely change your perceptions about money. In the Money Garden money does grow on trees.

> **"If you want to feel rich, just count the things you have that money cannot buy.**
>
> Proverb

EXERCISE

Sit yourself down in a comfy armchair, now think of a time when you felt really happy and had financial freedom.

Place your hand on your solar plexus 3"-4" above your navel and stay in this position feeling warm and safe.

Close your eyes and generate a picture of the time you were really happy and had financial freedom in your mind, bring in any sounds that you recall, or feelings, perhaps a certain taste or smell that you remember.

Experience the happy occasion fully in your mind, have you noticed any changes in your physiology? Have the memories you have put a smile on your face or made you laugh, have you straightened, or has your breathing changed?

I would imagine that your physiology has altered in some way. All I asked you to do was to recall the happy time; I did not ask you to change your physiology; however it will have changed in some way.

This little exercise reveals that the pictures, sounds, and so forth that you generated in your mind will have a huge influence on your physiology and as a consequence of this your choice of words, tonality of your voice and your behaviours will change.

Now stand up straight, look up to the ceiling and put a huge big smile on your face, breathe in for a count of 4 and hold for a count of 4 and breathe out for a count of 4. Now try to feel sad. I would imagine that you could not feel sad without shifting your physiology to a more depressed state, you have probably slumped your shoulders with your whole demeanour drooping.

This little exercise illustrates how your physiology influences your feelings whether positive or negative.

Next time you are feeling a little sad or upset try looking to the ceiling with your shoulders back and a smile on your face, you will not feel sad for long and you certainly will not be slumping your shoulders.

MONEY IS ROOT OF ALL EVIL?

Really think about this question, is money the root of all evil? Of course not, how can you ever think about enjoying financial freedom when you believe that money is the root of all evil?

When you think about the word money and the word evil, they equate to money-evil or evil money, this isn't good because your subconscious mind will automatically think that it is bad for you (evil-money) and therefore not let you have this evil money, because deep within you, there are these beliefs that money is the root of all evil.

ALL RICH PEOPLE ARE GREEDY AND TIGHT?

You are unintentionally clogging up your money pipes with your limiting fears and beliefs about money by thinking this way. The top and bottom of the matter is, money does not have the power to make a person greedy or bad, the money is simply energy, and energy follows thought. It is all about how you think and feel about money that makes a huge difference in life.

Becoming a greedy person is due to the greedy person's negative perception of money, and their motives about money. It is worth remembering, people who do not have a lot of money can be greedy and not have good intentions towards others. In life there is no exception to how people react when it comes down to money.

> There is only one class in the community that thinks more about money than the rich, and that is the poor.
>
> The poor can think of nothing else.
> Oscar Wilde

MONEY IS ENERGY

Money is energy and has to flow. When you hoard money, and put it away for a rainy day it isn't good because it isn't flowing. This is why the economic climate is in the state it is in. People stop spending money and that is stopping the flow of money. Shops and businesses close down because people hold on to their money and stop the flow. Money isn't scarce; it is that you perceive it to be scarce. There is abundance and prosperity for everyone, there always has been; it is just a matter of opening your mind to this fact.

KATE'S EXPERIENCE

Kate is a very special lady who learned that by going into 'The Money Garden' she could simply create anything her heart desired.

Kate came to see me a very frightened young lady. All her life had been based around fear, her fear was fear of everything, in particular men and the church. Because she was fearful, the vibrations that she was offering were ones of fear, consequently what was coming into her life were fear based people, situations, events and circumstances.

There were many personal issues about Kate's situation, many that I cannot mention. One thing in particular was that her husband had left her for someone else, leaving her with a huge amount of debt.

The girl could barely keep her head above water which is why in desperation she was referred to me by another client. Kate had so many outworn beliefs; one in particular was that 'money was the root of all evil'.

This negative view of money had been ingrained into her from being a child this is all that she knew. It is ludicrous to teach young people this; it can have such damaging effects on their lives. Kate thought that money was the root of all evil and, therefore, she didn't think she should have money which is why she didn't have any; which in turn created many problems affecting her health both mentally and physically.

> *Money, if it does not bring you happiness, will at least help you be miserable in comfort.*
> — Helen Gurley Brown

Her parents and siblings were the same and very judgemental about money; not only did they think that money was the root of all evil, they also had awful feelings within them towards people with money and had a tendency to look down on people who either had money or chose to seek it.

In this case I felt that Kate needed to be handled with kid gloves and I initially worked with her in 'The Releasing and Letting Go Garden', as to even suggest 'The Money Garden' she would have run a mile!

So because of the damaging beliefs she had, it took much longer than I originally thought it would for her to let go of the historically negative thoughts she had concerning money that had been indoctrinated over many years.

I explained to Kate that in life there are many things that she had to deal with moment by moment. There were things that she had control over and that she could change, and there were also things that she had no control over and therefore she had to accept that is the case and not waste any further energy on something that cannot be changed.

It is very important that all my clients and readers understand that you cannot change the past, do not waste any energy thinking about the negative things that have happened to you in the past, these may have been abusive or toxic relationships or a terrible event that has greatly affected your life.

What is important is that you realise you have the opportunity and power to change your life for the better not only now but for the rest of your life.

In Kate's situation taking her into 'The Releasing and Letting Go Garden' first we were able to let go of all her negative thoughts that had been indoctrinated in to her by her family as well as releasing and letting go the resentment she had from the hurt she still had from her relationship to her husband.

Once we had dealt with the releasing and letting go of Kate's negative past I explained to her that money is energy and many people from all walks of life may desire more money and energy in their life, it certainly does not mean that they are bad people.

Kate began to enter The Money Garden on a daily basis for over a year; she eventually managed to:

Pay off all of the debts left to her when her husband left.

She secured an excellent new job with a large company earning a great salary.

Took driving lessons and passed her test.

She bought a new car.

She bought a private number plate.

She bought out her husband's share in her house

She sold the house she shared with her husband and bought a stunning cottage.

She is so happy NOW!

She now knows and understands that money isn't evil; it can be put to some excellent uses. She is now very happy and one of the best manifesters I have ever met in my life!

You can be too!!!

Car sickness is the feeling you get when the monthly payment is due.
Author Unknown

THROUGH KATE VISITING THE UNIVERSAL MONEY GARDEN, SHE CHANGED HER LIFE BY EMBRACING THE FOLLOWING POINTS...

Accept the fact that there are things that can be changed; this is where you can release your unlimited potential!

Accept that there will be things beyond your control that cannot be changed, therefore do not exert or waste your precious 9 carat gold energy on what cannot be changed!

Accept that you are in control of your life.

Accept that you are not in control of anyone else's life.

The past is history and therefore you cannot go back, simply release it and let it go.

Understand that at any given moment in your life there are universal laws at work that are unwavering and always in action.

Know that the law of attraction is at work constantly, drawing to you situations, people, health, wealth and relationships into your life. This is reaping and sowing, you literally reap what you sow. What you give out is mirrored back to you moment by moment.

You have unlimited potential within you NOW to make important changes to how you live your life not only NOW but in the future.

The magic unfolds when you have true unwavering belief and faith, so step into the magic of believing and having blind unwavering faith NOW!

The only time that matters is NOW!

Actions and intentions are the key to all manifestation.

> To accomplish great things, we must not only act,
> but also dream; not only plan, but also believe.
>
> Anatole France

You are a bundle of intelligent energy and a manifester of all abundance when you put your mind to it. Working in the Money Garden helps you to work consciously, with focus on your thoughts and feelings of what your dreams and desires are.

The foundation of your dreams and desires is for you to discover and understand them, feel your dreams and desires to such an extent that your subconscious mind sees them to be reality, only then will that dream or desire become reality.

By deciding to enter 'The Universal Money Garden' you are clearing a path that if followed correctly will bring to you your dreams and desires in abundance, all you need to do is make that one simple decision to take that first step which will change your life.

What we really desire to do is what we are really meant to do.
When we do what we are meant to do, money comes to us,
doors open for us, we feel useful,
and the work we do feels like play to us.

Julia Cameron

The Money Garden...

Within The Money Garden
you will learn amongst other things how to...

Find out how much money you need and when you need it.

How to stop your money being frittered away
while manifesting even more money

Learn how to visualise and manifest money

Access 'The Universal Garden Bank'
where you will have a debit card with
an unlimited credit limit that is used in
The Universal Garden Banks ATM Machine.

"Our subconscious minds have no sense of humour, play no jokes and cannot tell the difference between reality and an imagined thought or image. What we continually think about eventually will manifest in our lives."
Robert Collier

THE LOVE GARDEN

Relates to the love of you, your spouse,
family and friends.
If you are lacking in this area,
this garden will help you to discover
the golden thread of love.

Gravitation is not responsible for people falling in love.
Albert Einstein

The Love Garden helps you to discover the real you within, with step-by-step instructions and daily exercises and affirmations.

The Love Garden is a wonderful tool for discovering the true golden thread of love within you.

THE LOVE GARDEN

The love garden is your saviour if you have ever experienced low self esteem, in yourself, life, or relationships. When you lack confidence and self esteem, you have a tendency to withdraw from many things, thinking and feeling, in that context, that you are not good enough, you are un-worthy.

THE LOVE GARDEN TEACHES YOU HOW TO...

Love You!

Love others with simplicity and trust!

Nurture your mind, body and spirit

Understand that there is no situation you cannot change in your life

Realise that nothing is beyond your ability

Treat yourself well

Accept total liability for your life and for what has gone on in it. Accept that events good or bad are all part of who you are, they are your make up and accepting them for what they are will help you change your life for the better.

> When people believe in themselves they have the first secret of success.
> Norman Vincent Peale

If you answer 'No' to any of the following questions your self esteem will be low and by going into 'The Love Garden' you will be making a huge positive impact on your well-being.

Question	Yes	No
Do you feel loveable?		
Do you love yourself?		
Do you find it easy to love others?		
When you look in the mirror do you like what you see?		
Do you have a great social life?		

If you answer yes to any of the following questions then again you will be suffering from low self esteem.

Question	Yes	No
Do you put yourself down in front of others?		
Do you hold back from trying things because you think that you are not good enough, or that there are other people that are better than you?		
Do you withdraw from society because you do not think that you fit in?		
Do you feel critical of you?		
Do you speak negatively about yourself to others?		

> We are each gifted in a unique and important way. It is our privilege and our adventure to discover our own special light.
>
> Mary Dunbar

DISCOVER HOW TO RELEASE YOUR INNER CRITIC

It is all about letting go of your inner critic, the inner voice that is forever judging you. Your self-esteem and self image are developed by how you internalise things, by talking to yourself with your inner voice. It becomes most prevalent when you are feeling down.

The Love Garden offers tools and techniques ensuring that there are very few down days if any at all, but when those down days raise their ugly head you will be able to deal with them in an optimistic and positive way.

ARE YOU ON THE TREADMILL OF LIFE?

The tools and techniques in the Love Garden help you to analyse your inner critical thoughts, determining the thoughts, and how these thoughts make you feel. Self critical thoughts keep you stuck in a rut, unable to move forward, going nowhere on the treadmill of life. The Love Garden teaches you how to release and set yourself free from the treadmill of life with those outdated patterns, worn out beliefs, fears that have held you back for so long from the realisation of the real you within.

YOU ARE A CO-CREATOR OF YOUR LOVE LIFE!

You are a co-creator of your life manifesting what you place your focus on the most. If you think and feel that your ideal love partner is eluding you then they will. The Love Garden guides you to becoming an influential co-creator of not only your love life but every area of your life; transforming it with step-by-step tools and information.

THE LOVE GARDEN WILL...

Offer specific techniques for receiving your desires of love and happiness

Teach you how to turn your dreams into reality by manifesting the love of your life

Teach you essential ingredients to harness the love of attraction

Teach you how to see obstacles as stepping stones to meet the love of your life with hands on tools

Teach you how to use the law of attraction to work miracles in your life

Teach you to fully understand the magical tool of the love of attraction.

The Love Garden helps you to discover the real you within, with step-by-step instructions and daily exercises and affirmations. The Love Garden is a wonderful tool for discovering the true golden thread of love within you. The Love Garden guides you with motivational style, looking deep within you, discovering potentiality you didn't know you had.

DAVID'S STORY

When David came to my therapy practice, he was a very gifted professional with a very successful career; he had moved from Ireland to the Lake District in 2005 and is still living there now. He really came over as a genuinely nice man; you are probably thinking why David was coming to see me; as he has a great career, money and along with all that a decent person?

However, when he first came to see me he didn't view himself in that way at all, all David saw was someone staring back at him through the mirror that he didn't really like.

He really wished to see himself as the successful chap he was, however because David had been brought up in a children's home and was always being told that he was ugly, and would never make anything of himself, it was not just a barrier in his life, it was a great immovable boulder. He really was struggling to move past these obstacles in his life.

If when in the young stages of life you are not supported, it can be very damaging in later life as it is at this stage our building blocks are being formed. As a boy David was ignored, and criticised on a daily basis, his foundations were weak and therefore he continued to criticise himself as he grew older.

As he grew up, his belief was that he wasn't worthy of having solid relationships. In a way it was a catalyst to him being successful as he threw himself into his business life, leaving no time for anything or anyone else. In fact how he has such an amazing business is astonishing, bearing in mind the mental cruelty he went through.

David was in my therapy clinic for one thing, to have a happy, loving, secure relationship and raise a family; he simply wanted the one thing that he had never had, a loving family life.

I very soon discovered that David had little self esteem, even though he was a very successful business man, he really didn't own any self confidence.

He did not view himself as most successful people do; he held beliefs that he was ugly, and without any personality. He thought he needed a personality transplant as well as a whole new face. David's inner critic distorted his whole perception of himself and what he was really all about. For David, his negative self-talk became his daily inner dialogue.

David really had to begin to like himself, even if it was only a teeny weenie bit. So I had a huge task ahead of me! We began with coaching and NLP for 3 weeks before we progressed to 'The Love Garden'.

Being a stereotypical man, he thought The Love Garden was about relationships and Valentine Day romances, which it can be, but, The Love Garden is more often than not about you loving yourself. Your life is all about how you value yourself; who you are and what you are about is essential.

I asked David if he knew the George Benson song 'Greatest love of all' which he didn't, so I sang these few words from the song to him" the greatest love of all, is easy to achieve, learning to love yourself, is the greatest love of all". David filled up, I wasn't sure if it was my singing or the words, thankfully it was the words.

I explained to David that the Love Garden would help him to discover the more he learned to love himself, the more love he could and would give to others. People love people who love and respect themselves, the more a person loves and respect themselves the more others will wish to respond to them. The Love Garden is a total win-win situation, learning to love yourself firstly results in that person beginning to be loved by others, which in turn benefits not just their life but everyone who come into contact with that person.

David eventually came around to the concept of The Love Garden, and proceeded to go into the garden every day. He found the balloon and candle technique to be of huge benefit, the affirmation cards and the subconscious re-programming to be a huge benefit; in fact looking back now he says that those techniques transformed his perception of himself. After three months of being in the garden everyday David said that he felt a huge shift in how he felt about himself, he realised that he was a good and decent person that he was successful but more importantly people around him greatly respected his success and he felt proud about his achievements.

He was starting to like himself and love himself; we worked continually on filling his heart with love for himself. Of course we were making great progress but David still had that one thing missing that he so wished; a loving relationship.

He asked how he could do this, I advised him to make room for his new partner, by making some room for her in his life. Remember David was a seasoned bachelor with his own bachelor routines, for David to attract a partner into his life he had to literally make room for that person in his life!

I told him to make space in his wardrobes and draws for her clothes, sleep on either the left or the right hand side of the bed, and not in the middle (if you choose the right side only sleep on the right side}, park his car so that his future love has room to park her car, write affirmations that included the new love in his life now, however more than anything feel the love within himself!

David was a model client; he listened to everything, did as I asked him to do, he trusted me and embraced the whole process. After six months of being my client and working in The Love Garden, he confessed to me in one session in a very shy way, that he loved himself and was very proud of his achievements and was now ready for romance.

David found the love of his life Hazel, and they married. He now has a loving relationship to make his great life complete. Only by David firstly being able to like and love himself was he able to attract love into his life,

The Love Garden is such a powerful tool to help this process take place.

I love a happy ending!

The Love Garden...

Within The Love Garden
you will learn amongst other things how to...

Discover the golden thread of love within you.

Discover 'The Love Genie' with his lamp, for you to rub and
bring all your loving desires into being.

Begin liking and loving yourself.

Learn to attract the love of your life.

Plant your loving seeds in your personal seed map.

Discover your own mantra to attract true love.

Bathe in The Fountain of Love.

By deciding to move into 'The Universal Love Garden'
you are opening the doors to an amazing world of love,
enlightenment and true appreciation of true love in your life;
all you have to do is have the courage
to walk through that door.

Having a low opinion of you is not "modesty".
It's self-destruction.
Holding your uniqueness in high regard is not "egotism",
it's a necessary precondition to happiness and success.
Bobbe Sommer

THE GOALS AND DESIRES GARDEN

Relates to you discovering what your
true goals and desires are in life;
as well as showing you how to achieve them.

The road leading to a goal
does not separate you from the destination;
it is essentially a part of it.
Charles De-Lint

As you constantly think a thought over and over in your head, that thought manifests into a habit good or bad.

If you have set goals and you have not achieved them, fear not!

The Goals and Desires Garden will come to your rescue.

THE GOALS AND DESIRES GARDEN

Do you ever set goals and desires that you wish to achieve? If you do not then you should!

If you have set goals and you have not achieved them, fear not The Goals and Desires Garden will come to your rescue.

Setting goals for yourself is the first step towards achieving those goals. We should all have a plan of action in life as it gives us something to work towards. If you do not take the first step of setting your goal, further action for achieving your goal simply will not happen.

Everyone knows someone who does not possess any va va voom in their day to day life, they will have a very dutiful approach towards life; where nothing magical happens and more importantly they assume that what you get dealt in life is what you have to put up with for the rest of your life.

Unfortunately, these people seem to aimlessly drift through life in their own little world. Many of them work really hard, harder than they need to in some cases. They never seem to achieve anything worthwhile but assume life is tough and that it always will be tough.

I may have just described you and your life? Well, the good news is by buying this book you have shown that you do not want to live your life like that forever. In fact by reading this book you have started on a path that will change how you look at your life for the better.

The reason that many are submissive towards life is because they have not put their mind to thinking about what they truly desire from life, having not formed any goals. Setting goals for yourself means that you are planting your destiny seed; have belief that the destiny seedling will sprout and establish itself and grow into your desire.

.

When you do not set any goals for you to achieve, you wander through life, moment by moment, day by day with nothing to aim for. This means that in twelve months time from now, your life will be the same as it is now, it will basically be the same, except for a few minor changes that are probably not down to you, the changes will be what others have achieved for you

Yes of course there are times in your life where you feel powerless of change, when you feel like you are stuck in a rut. You feel knee deep in responsibilities and have trouble making any progress in changing things and therefore have little or no passion and purpose.

Feeling stuck in a rut arises when you are literally emotionally and physically in a cycle of depravation, worry, and fear, it is as though you are up to your chest in quicksand and going deeper and deeper.

Your thoughts take up space in your mind and when this space is filled with outdated, feeble and unproductive thoughts it is impossible to fill it with new and productive thoughts because is overcrowded with old, fragile, useless ones, similar to a computer your thought memory is full.

To help free some of that memory go into The Goals and Desires Garden for mental house cleaning where you release all the unproductive stale thoughts and replace with vibrant, positive and optimistic ones.

Many people are ingrained with arrays of habits many of which are negative and it is these habits that restrict your growth and development. As you constantly think a thought over and over in your head, that thought manifests into a habit good or bad.

> Role models set goals for you
> and try to make you as good as they are.
> Role models are important.
> Kasey Zacharias

Go into the Garden of Goals and Desires garden, where you will be given specific tools and techniques to set goals and reach them easily.

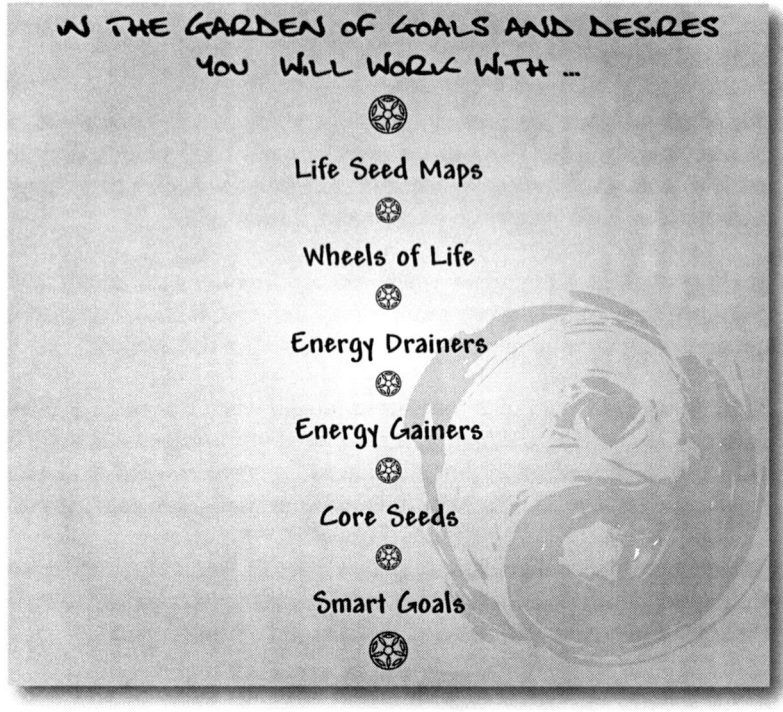

Consequently, once you begin achieving the goals and desires in the garden you will discover a confidence to move on and set more advanced ones.

If you cannot visualise yourself accomplishing your goal, the odds are you will not achieve it. Seeing your goal in your mind's eye is believing in your goal. It will definitely help if you can keep a picture of your desire with you at all times, so that you are reminded of it every day; this might be a photo of your dream home, car or job.

GOAL SETTING AND A POSITIVE FRAME OF MIND

If you do not have the correct approach to setting your goal, it can have a serious downside.

Incorrect goal setting will undermine your success.

Incorrect goal setting makes you unable to concentrate your actions and energy where required, consequently you will become disillusioned.

If you execute your goal for wrong reasons, it will have a significant negative impact.

In the Garden of Goals and Desires you understand that seeing is believing.

SETTING AND ATTAINING GOALS.

Did you know that you will achieve your goals if you focus on them one at a time?

Once you have achieved your goal you can then begin working on your next goal.

Choose 1 small goal, and be specific about your goal.

Did you know that larger goals can be broken down into small chunks (interim goals) that can be completed on a daily basis?

Keep a record every day: this step is vital in achieving your goals! You will never achieve your goals if you do not keep a record of your daily growth.

Make your goal a habit, just like cleaning your teeth.

Although we may start small our aim is to eventually think big, because big successes begin with small successes.

Did you know that if you have any kind of doubt, uncreative thoughts, and words, these will stop your goals in its tracks?

LISA'S EXPERIENCE OF GOAL SETTING

A client of mine came to me for life coaching, I quickly realised that Lisa was a little like a butterfly flitting from one thing to another never pausing to think about one thing in particular before something else caught her attention and she flitted off to that.

By leading her life like this she never seemed to achieve anything as before she finished a project or task she would leave and start another project and before that was finished she would start something else; it was a never ending cycle of failure and disappointment.

So it was a bit of a culture shock that I set Lisa one goal and one goal only, to learn to meditate.

I took Lisa into The Garden of Goals and Desires; it took a little while for Lisa to settle as thought after thought after thought kept popping into her mind.

The conscious mind thinks it is in control and does not like you to slow your mind down to just an individual thought. The conscious mind can think of several things at once, however it can only perform one task at a time, so for Lisa to clear her mind she had to still her mind.

I asked Lisa to set an intention in motion to always be present in the moment. She found this difficult as she thought there were more things to do than just being present in the moment.

The mind is where all your experiences firstly begin, through a thought and from that thought it is brought into reality and experience.

Like Lisa, when you are new to goal setting and setting intentions; your mind can be likened to Niagara Falls with your thoughts tumbling over like gushing water; so many of them at such high speed and volume your mind cannot make head nor tail of them. You need to slow your mind down so that your thoughts run like a gentle stream rather than an out of control rampaging torrent, through this calm and profound peace your conscious mind can start to make sense of these thoughts.

Lisa set her intention and set her goal to still her mind three times a day for two minutes.

She went into The Goals and Desires Garden everyday for thirty days and began to really focus her mind, she not only focused her mind she actually mastered her mind.

Through going into the Goals and Desires Garden everyday for a minimum of thirty days your mind eventually accepts the control that you have over it, your mind no longer runs like Niagara Falls; but starts understanding and processing each thought in a calm and organised way. Lisa now makes meditation a part of her calm and organised life where she sets goals for her desires and more importantly achieves them before setting further goals.

By taking one small step you can too, visit The Goals and Desires Garden.

The journey of a thousand miles begins with a single step.
Lao-tzu

Exercise to Set Your Personal Goal

Setting goals is an influential way for envisioning your perfect future and for motivating yourself to turn your dreams into reality. Your dreams and desires are intentions and the fuel for your goals. Writing down your dreams and desires in black and white, you are in fact setting a goal or goals with the intention of achieving them.

When writing down your goals ensure that they are smart goals. Smart goals are specific, measureable, achievable, realistic and within a time frame to achieve your dreams and desires, they are your priority 'to do' list.

Example:
If you wish to be in a position where you always have £1000 put away for emergencies or a rainy day but there is no way that you would have £1000 spare to put away; you must look at this goal in an achievable way.
If saving £1000 is daunting then you need to break this down into interim goals.

So, how much would you have to save a month over a year to have that £1000? The answer is £83.33, still a bit of a struggle but more manageable than £1000.

So, how much would you have to save a week to save that £1000? The answer is £19.23 that seems a lot easier than £83.33 a month.

So, how much would you have to save a day to save that £1000? The answer is £2.74, now that is achievable!

At the end of the year you will have that £1000 put away for a rainy day and the reason it is there is because you gave yourself interim goals that felt achievable.

Always make sure that all your goals are SMART goals.
S = Specific
M = Measureable
A = Achievable
R = Realistic
T = Time Frame

EXERCISE TO SET YOUR PERSONAL GOAL

Identify the goals that you desire to accomplish

❁

You then break your goal down into interim goals

❁

You now have to take action to achieve these goals within the time frame set

❁

Once you have successfully achieved your goal be happy, be grateful, and enjoy the achievement of achieving your goal. Remember to show gratitude for how you have moved on in life being an achiever.

The Goals and Desires Garden...

**Within The Goals and Desires Garden
you will learn amongst other things..**

**How to set and complete your goals perfectly in the time frame
you set, with confidence, and a great sense of accomplishment**

**How you will change your life by learning
how to change your mind**

**How, by setting sharp, clearly defined goals,
you'll see forward progress in what might previously
have seemed a long pointless grind**

How setting goals will lift your self-confidence

**How you will recognise your own skill and ability
in setting and achieving your goals**

**How you will discover the GOLDEN KEY
to goal setting and achieving your goals.**

The ability to convert ideas to things
is the secret to outward success.
Henry Ward Beecher

THE GUARDIAN ANGEL GARDEN

Relates to you discovering your personal
Guardian Angel that has been with you on
your journey from birth until your death.
This garden will help you to identify and
make contact with your Angel;
enhancing not only your life but your Guardian Angels too.

**Thorns and stings and those things,
just make stronger, our angel wings.**
Terri Guillemets

You may be cautious or even scared of finding out and working with your Guardian Angel.

I cannot stress strongly enough how much love, protection and guidance you will receive once you have committed yourself to entering The Guardian Angel Garden.

Your Guardian Angel is with you now, looking over you and protecting you; now is the time to get to know him.

THE GUARDIAN ANGEL GARDEN

Do Guardian Angels really exist?

Not only do they exist, they are your best friend and always by your side since the day you were born. Go into The Guardian Angel Garden and discover how they watch over you, loving and caring for you at all times until your passing.

Your Guardian Angels eyes are always permanently fixed upon you. When you walk your Guardian Angel walks with you. When you stop, your Guardian Angel also stops; when you go to sleep your Guardian Angel watches over you protecting and loving you ensuring that no harm comes to you. Always remember that you have nothing to fear because you always have and always will have the protection and guidance of your beloved Guardian Angel.

> **Guardian Angels are ethereal divine beings that are assigned to individuals here on Earth on their journey of life.**
> Grace Brown

THE TOUCH OF YOUR GUARDIAN ANGEL

There are many occasions that are frequently put down to fate, chance or even a miracle; however they all have the touch of a hand of ethereal light behind it. Your astonishing Guardian Angel walks right beside your side every day.

Your Guardian Angels assist you more than you will ever know. You will have experienced times where you literally acted on your gut instinct, it is during this random time where all logic goes out of the window and the gut instinct kicks in, well this is your Guardian Angel guiding you to do the right thing in that precise moment.

Go into the Guardian Angel Garden and discover your intuitive Guardian Angel and ask to be shown what you are meant to do on this journey of life.

CONNECTING WITH YOUR GUARDIAN ANGEL?

Connecting with your Guardian Angel is a celebration for your life and their existence.

HOW TO GET THE MOST FROM YOUR GUARDIAN ANGEL

The Guardian Angel Garden helps you to connect
with your Guardian Angel and for him to:

Celebrate your life and times with you

Experience great times of happiness with you

Celebrate your coming of age

Celebrate your wedding with you

Take care of you when you or your spouse gives birth

Always remember that your Guardian Angel
is here to celebrate your life with you.

> We're all kissed by angels
> but some of us never think to pucker.
> Terri Guillemets

DO GUARDIAN ANGELS MAKE THEIR PRESENCE KNOWN?

You may hear whispers, angelic chimes or the gentle sound of a harp, or in my case it has always been the very gentle tinkle of bells; all these sounds are ways that your Guardian Angel make their presence known. They also make their presence known by a feeling of warmth or comfort, again for me it has always been a tingling, or, should you be suffering more upsetting feelings like grief or sadness, they will very gently tuck you under their cloak of feathered wings, wrapping them around you, giving you unconditional love and compassion until you feel a little better. When I sit quietly I ask for my head to be stroked, and it always is beautifully.

Why do not you discover the Guardian Angel Garden and learn how to contact and ask your Guardian Angel for help? You will be astonished how quickly you will learn the answers to your questions, and how easily things begin happening for you.

You do not have to be religious or spiritual to learn about Guardian Angels. The only thing that you require to identify the angels is to be open and receptive, and be aware as the angels catch you off guard and surprise you.

> **The wings of angels are often found on the backs of the least likely people.**
> Eric Honeycutt

Love and Your Guardian Angel

We all have the golden thread of love running through us because love is what you and I are composed of. It was love that created the universe. Going into The Guardian Angel Garden you will discover your golden thread of love running through you, feeling and encompassing of love, for you and for those around you, for those who matter and make a difference to your life.

The Angels will always let you know that you are always loved and never alone which is a wonderful gift. The Guardian Angel Garden will assist in you firstly learning to love yourself and to love others with the same all encompassing love that they offer to you.

Encompassing love in the Guardian Angel Garden can cover a great distance.

> Your Guardian Angel can offer love and security
> in your personal world.
>
> Your feeling of safety will stem from what you believe.
> Your Guardian Angel will help you to change perceptions
> that are clouding your judgement at present.
>
> To have the security of knowing that your Guardian Angel
> is keeping a watchful eye over you helps you
> feel safe and secure.
>
> Your Guardian Angel loves you unconditionally 100%
>
> Your Guardian Angel will always offer you
> encouragement and support

> **Life is a tapestry:**
> **We are the warp; angels, the weft; God, the weaver.**
> **Only the Weaver sees the whole design.**
> Eileen Elias Freeman

Your Guardian Angel is your best friend always has been and always will be.

Your Guardian Angels oversee everything in your life including your relationships in your everyday life.

IN THE GUARDIAN ANGEL GARDEN YOU CAN...

Ask for healing love around your current relationship

Ask for a relationship to come to an end and for healing for the highest good of everyone concerned

Ask for love to enter your life

Ask for a loving partner or your current partner or spouse to be more loving

Ask for a new circle of friends

Ask for healing love amongst your working colleagues

The Guardian Angel Garden offers a complete way of working with spiritual relationship transformation, with emphasis on the true and authentic you.

Your Guardian Angels oversee your relationships in your everyday life.
Grace Brown

FORGIVENESS IN THE ANGEL GARDEN

Your Guardian Angel always wishes you to have forgiveness in your heart, it is essential in leading a healthy positive life. Your guardian Angel helps you to release the negativity of resentment and thoughts of revenge. Forgiveness will allow you to focus positivity in your life. Your Guardian Angel guides you to feelings of understanding, empathy and compassion for the offender who wounded you.

Being unforgiving and holding on to feelings of bitterness and anger can cause serious problems to your health and well-being. When you hold onto feelings of bitterness and anger, you will be suffering poor health. This is because you are holding on to such negative feelings that cause you to encounter a weakened immune system which eventually can lead to a chronic illness such as cancer.

Research shows that cancer can be the result of being unforgiving and being in a constant state of chronic unforgiveness. If you learn to forgive in The Guardian Angel Garden your immune system will be strengthened, cortisol levels will be reduced and you will experience lower levels of chronic pain and less stress.

If you would like to release yourself from being un-forgiving then go into The Guardian Angel Garden and commit to a process of change.

The golden moments in the stream of life rush past us
and we see nothing but sand;
the angels come to visit us,
and we only know them when they are gone.
George Elliot

RELEASING YOUR FEAR TO YOUR GUARDIAN ANGEL

If you worry about terrible things that have not happened to you yet but you worry they might, or you worry that history may repeat itself. Or, if you are generally pessimistic then by going into The Guardian Angel Garden you can allow your Guardian Angel to help in removing your fears.

If you are a fearful person, The Guardian Angel Garden is the place for you to be.

THE GUARDIAN ANGEL GARDEN WILL HELP YOU REALISE...

Fear of the unfamiliar is a powerful driving force

Fear will always restrict you and hold you back

Fear keeps you stuck in the same place with the same people, relationships, career and even down to where you live

Fear offers you no future

Fear will destroy what courage and initiative you have

Fear of the unknown is one of society's ways of keeping you under control.

When you go into The Guardian Angel Garden your Guardian Angel will help you to overcome your fears by teaching you that faith is the key. Your Guardian Angel will enlighten you to know that faith in the ultimate realisation of your hopes and desires.

> Your Guardian Angel is by your side always,
> forever and a day through eternity, love, laugh and love.
>
> Grace Brown

The Guardian Angel Garden...

Within The Guardian Angel Garden
you will learn amongst other things how...

You will learn how to ask for a message

✦

To be open and receptive to your question being answered

✦

To understand your Guardian Angel

✦

You will learn how to communicate with your Guardian Angel

✦

To establish regular contact with your Guardian Angel

To learn from your guardian angels

✦

Angels descending, bring from above,
Echoes of mercy, whispers of love.
Fanny J. Crosby

THE HEALING GARDEN

Relates to the health and well being of your life.
You will find that true healing occurs
at source level in this garden.

The greatest wealth is health.
Virgil

It is in the Healing Garden you will discover how to remove your self-imposed blocks to complete realisation and eternal joy.

The Healing Garden offers you practices for healing that will enable you to deal steadily and positively with adversity that you may encounter in your everyday life.

THE HEALING GARDEN

> Healing is a matter of time,
> but it is sometimes also a matter of opportunity.
> Hippocrates

WHAT IS THE HEALING GARDEN?

If you would like to experience healing and harmony, peace and well-being in your life then The Healing Garden is the place to be. It is an amazing place with powerful techniques that work literally at the source level of what requires healing; it is wonderful to realise how much healing you can expect.

Your mind, conscious and subconscious has the ability to in effect process, analyse and use the vast amount of information that surrounds you. It is always learning and adapting new commands and challenges, expanding further than perceived limitations.

It is your subconscious mind that regulates and influences your physiological functions. We work very much on the subconscious mind in The Healing Garden with conscious repetitive reprogramming.

It is in the Healing Garden you will discover how to remove your self-imposed blocks to complete realisation and eternal joy.

Simply, The Healing Garden offers you practices for healing that will enable you to deal steadily and positively with adversity that you may encounter in your everyday life.

> Healing takes courage, and we all have courage,
> even if we have to dig a little to find it.
> Tori Amos

WHAT YOU THINK AFFECTS YOUR HEALTH?

Without your health you are scuppered as health is a vital aspect of your life. But, wrongly many people tend to take their health for granted. When your health is good, you are probably multi tasking, juggling plates, managing to keep all the plates balancing in the air at the same time, you do not even consider your health. When you are not feeling too good, it knocks your socks off, it affects everything in your life, your relationships, your career, everything.

There is a great deal of scientific evidence regarding how the mind affects the body. The evidence indicates that our mind and our emotions influence illness. Positive and negative ingrained beliefs within the mind are replicated in other parts of the body.

It is important that you understand that your beliefs, positive or negative, affect your health. Your belief system is a powerful part of your being. It dictates who you are and what you represent, both mentally and physically. Your belief system is formed by how you perceive things.

When your subconscious mind accepts your perceptions, whether they are true or false, positive or negative, they literally become part of your belief system and eventually become your reality.

It is important that you realise, you are what you think you are!

If you think that you are successful, then you will be, if you think you are a failure then you will be, likewise if you think you are constantly unhealthy then guess what?

> **If you think you can do it, or you think you cannot do it, you are right.**
> Henry Ford

RELEASING UNSOLVED EMOTIONS

The healing garden has techniques that are invaluable for your healing, that help you to release the unsolved emotion, and bring about the magic of healing.

If you think about illness, it is a last resort to get your attention. Your subconscious mind has probably been sending you warning signs that you have been unaware of or have decided to ignore.

Healing yourself in the Healing Garden is easy and yet extremely effective. The healing process in The Healing Garden allows you to connect to what is happening to you physically and emotionally, uncovering your unsolved emotions and once discovering those emotions releasing them for the healing to occur. It is a remarkable journey of healing, releasing entrenched layers of worry, anger and fear in order to heal the mind and body.

The Healing Garden is a way of true peace and healing that creates spiritual wisdom, bringing about personal and spiritual radiance.

It brings out a new form of consciousness within you that reawakens your spirit, bringing about spiritual growth and development.

New opportunities will open up to you, making it possible for you to reach your highest potential.

> Just as the body cannot exist without blood, so the soul needs the matchless and pure strength of faith.
> Mahatma Gandhi

WHAT ARE ENERGY DRAINERS?

When your energy is drained by another person we call them energy drainers. In their presence you feel lethargic, tired, irritable and run down. This is not good for your personal health and well-being and must be dealt with as soon as you become aware that this is happening to you.

Many of us are kind and caring people and because of that fact put up with what is being thrown at us, seemingly accepting what is thrown at us as opposed to repairing the damage.

The Healing Garden offers tools and techniques to discover, who, where and what are your energy drainers.

There can be many energy drainers in your life that drain your life force out of you. Your energy drainer quite often is a person but can also be your work place or your home. Energy drainers literally drain your energy leaving you feeling deflated and lifeless, a little like when a vampire sucks away all of the blood leaving the person lifeless.

It would be amazing to eradicate or totally avoid those, who or what zaps your energy; however before you can eradicate them you have to discover what, where and who the drainers are.

People who drain you emotionally and mentally tend to have real issues or problems in their own lives, combined with the fact that energy drainers can also be quite controlling results in a potentially negative concoction. Energy draining people tend to endure emotional problems and never seem to improve their lives in anyway and seem to thrive on that fact.

Eventually you will come to understand that love heals everything, and love is all there is.
Gary Zukav

Here is a list of examples of energy drainers at home and at work.

Energy Drainers at Home	Energy Drainers at Work
The bed is never made when I arrive home	Anne who I sit next to sighs all of the time
The pots are still in the sink from the last nights meal	Tony moans about never having any money
I don't have any clean clothes, I did not do any washing last week	Allison keeps whispering she does not like our boss
The stairs are filthy	My boss is very critical
The kitchen cupboard is crammed with unopened mail	Helen sounds as though she is crying every time she speaks to me
There are piles of old papers and magazines stuffed in a corner	Mary talks all the time about how ill her sister is
The bathroom is desperately in need of a clean	My office chair is broken and uncomfortable
My neighbours are always arguing	It is so hot and the windows have to remain closed
The neighbour across the road is always complaining about the parking	No one seems to answer the phone except me
The grass needs cutting, in fact the garden is a mess	I always stay late to catch up with my work

As you can see in the above examples most of the energy drainers are easily corrected when in the home while at work you may have more of a problem addressing some of the energy drainers. The majority of the energy drainers at home are dealt with fairly easily by a bit of organisation and husbandry.

If you have a partner or spouse sit down with them and work out a rota so that you share the chores between you. All of these energy drainers in the home apart from the two concerning the neighbours are simply dealt with by using organisation, commitment and effort. Once you have dealt with these problems you will immediately start to feel more energized with a much more positive outlook on life generally.

If you are in the fortunate position to afford to hire the services of a gardener or a cleaner and this works well for you, then do not hesitate as you will be still dealing with those energy drainers in a positive way and will still benefit from them being negated.

Regarding your neighbours who are always arguing and the neighbour across the road who is always complaining about the parking; you have to distance yourself from these situations.

When next speaking to your neighbour and he or she starts to moan about the parking situation; do not comment on the subject and move onto some other subject; your neighbour will start to realise that you are not interested in the subject resulting in you not adding petrol to the fire.

Regarding the neighbours who argue frequently, this is a tough one. In the short term you could move to another area of your house; if it persists you have to address the situation by perhaps sending them a card explaining your predicament, if they are reasonable people it should have a positive effect; but sometimes there is only one solution to a problem like this and that is to move.

Although this sounds extreme, remember energy drainers can be very toxic and it is essential to your wellbeing that you address them.

Literally all of the negative drainers at work seem to be negative people and their problems; forever complaining, or having constant dramas. People who are energy drainers or energy vampires count on other people being caring and kind who offer them the attention or approval they are seeking.

Again you have to distance yourself from these people; I know at work this can be difficult especially when one of them is your boss. So, by going into The Healing Garden you will find ways of dealing with the energy drainers, for the present time I would strongly advice that in order of stopping your energy being drained, you must fully accept that you are not responsible for anyone else's feelings except for your own.

Accepting that you are only responsible for you and no one else will determine that you can subtly move away from any negative draining associations.

If from the example you find yourself in a situation that there are so many different energy drainers affecting you then it may be time to look for a new job; if you do not you will be opening yourself up to stress and illness.

The first thing to do is find who or what energy drainers are in your life.

Fill in the table below, state all of the energy drainers in your home and workplace, please be honest with yourself, list what, where and who drains you.

Energy Drainers at Home	Energy Drainers at Work

Now that you have listed your personal energy drainers, you should now be in a position to address them in a positive constructive way.

If you have highlighted untidy areas in your home; as stated previously sit down with your partner or spouse and instigate a plan between you that is achievable and workable. If you live at home by yourself then give yourself a longer period to address these areas.

If you have identified certain people in your life who are energy vampires it is advisable that you spend as little time in their company as possible. Try this simple exercise which will help bring about perfect health.

EXERCISE

This is a very quick and easy exercise to understand and enjoy;
it will totally enlighten your awareness to healing yourself.

Sitting down quietly and being consciously aware is a profoundly powerful act.
Thinking about your perfect health several times a day and having the belief that you are going to achieve perfect health will eventually invoke perfect health within you.
By simply focusing your thoughts on perfect health you are not only setting the healing process in motion you are also planting a seed to nurture your perfect health.

Because we plant thought seeds moment by moment it is so important that you nurture these seeds, resulting in perfect health.

Find somewhere where you can sit upright for 5 minutes undisturbed.
Sit down with your spine straight.
Take off your shoes and undo any tight clothing.
Breathe in slowly on a count of 4, holding in for a count of 4 and exhale slowly on a count of 4. Repeat 4 times.

Now, for a period of 60 seconds, speak out loud the following affirmation - "I have perfect health and well-being thank you"

Focus only on the words you are reciting, any thoughts and images that come in to the mind, pay them no attention, simply focus on the words of the affirmation.

You should be able to recite this affirmation around 20 times during the 60 seconds, depending on how quickly you speak it.

Feel perfect health in your entire being, feel in your whole body the healing beginning to occur.

If you try this little exercise several times a day everyday it will eventually drop into your subconscious mind, giving you the belief of perfect health.

The Healing Garden…

Within The Healing Garden
you will learn amongst other things how to…

Learn to understand the mind, body and spirit connection
to your health and well-being and how to
release disrupted or stuck energy

Be given insight into how your thoughts develop into your
words and those words become your actions,
those actions will eventually become your habits and
your habits will eventually constitute who you become

Identify powerful self-healing techniques that you can use
each and every day in The Healing Garden

Discover what lower vibrating energies are, how to release
them, leaving you feeling healthy with a positive well-being

Learn that perfect health is your divine right and how
manifesting perfect health becomes second nature to you

Discover amazing tools and techniques to find who,
where and what are your energy drainers
and how to quickly eliminate them.

Your lifestyle - how you live, eat, emote, and think - determines your health.
To prevent disease, you may have to change how you live.

Brian Carter

THE DREAMS AND ASPIRATIONS GARDEN

Relates to your dreams and aspirations,
this garden will show you not just how to raise them
but also how to achieve them.

Dreams are illustrations...
from the book your soul is writing about you.
Marsha Norman

In The Dreams and Aspirations Garden you can reach for the stars.

I ask you to always expect the best, and be patient.

Your biggest success is waiting for you in The Garden of Dreams and Aspirations.

Discover it now.

THE DREAMS AND ASPIRATIONS GARDEN

What is your Dream and what do you aspire to?

Your subconscious mind is your faithful servant and whatever your Dreams or Aspirations are; once they are programmed into your subconscious mind your faithful servant will fulfil.

Your subconscious mind is the one who calls the shots, no one else; your subconscious is in total charge of your Dreams and Aspirations.

But, it is important to realise, it is not only your Dreams and Aspirations that it draws to you, your Subconscious Mind can also draw to you negative situations and dilemmas that you could well do without.

Why is this so, I hear you cry? It all depends on how and what your subconscious mind has been programmed and ingrained with since childhood.

If you are fortunate to have consistent optimistic good thoughts then that is what your subconscious mind will assume you must have drawn to you; optimistic and good people and situations. Likewise if you suffer from ingrained negative and bad thoughts then again your subconscious mind will dutifully attract negative or bad situations and people into your life.

The Dreams and Aspiration Garden coaches you to nurture good thoughts through repetition to re-programme your subconscious mind. It also trains you to add emotion to your Dreams and Aspirations bringing a speedy conclusion to you desired outcome. You will not only create and love this garden you will also flourish in it!

> We cannot become what we want to be
> by remaining what we are.
> Max DePree

ARE YOU AFRAID TO DREAM BIG?

Are you afraid to dream BIG, and stretch your thinking? Is it because you do not know what you wish to dream BIG about? Do your dreams and desires appear unattainable pie in the sky stuff, making you feel uncomfortable or unsure?

The Garden of Dreams and Aspirations coaches you to dream BIG turning your dreams into your reality. The Garden will uncover your potential deep within you. Releasing your unlimited potential gives you power of your personal growth.

In The Garden of Dreams and Aspirations you learn how to tap into your hidden potentiality through the use of remarkable, journalling, seed maps, visualisation, affirmations and individual tools and techniques specifically for this garden. In the Garden of Dreams and Aspiration, everything that you can possibly imagine is possible and waiting for you.

Your true potential is far greater than you could ever imagine.

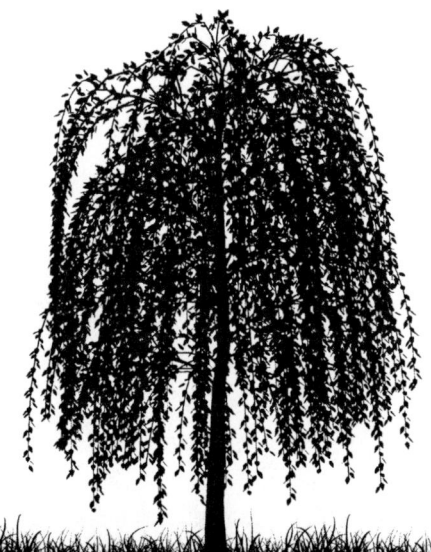

WOULD YOU LIKE TO MOVE OUT OF YOUR COMFORT ZONE?

The Dreams and Aspiration Garden will help you to you feel comfortable when stepping out of your comfort zone.

The Dreams and Aspiration Garden shows you how your comfort zone formulates your thinking patterns, your home and work environments, family and friends and establishes how you live your life. Many people remain in their comfort zone all their lives, through having the fear of moving out of that zone they invariably never reach their true potential. The journey that takes you out of your comfort zone is a road that is not travelled much as it challenges your beliefs and expands the boundaries of what feels comfortable to you.

All of us invariably come to a T Junction in life where one way is comfort zone village wrapped in a security blanket of Mr and Mrs Average; whereas the other direction leads to Dreams and Aspirations City, where you are open to the hugely positive elements of achievement, success and wonderment.

Now, I am not knocking people who are happy with their lot in life and for staying in their comfort zone it is their decision and I respect it.

But, if you do not want to live your life in this way then having the courage to step out of that comfort zone is essential. You will initially suffer discomfort as change is not easy to deal with, it is alien to what your subconscious mind thinks is natural; your subconscious mind will always try and haul you back to your comfort zone whenever you step out of it.

Complacency is the greatest enemy of creativity and future success; for you to stretch and grow you have to feel uncomfortable.

By going into The Dreams and Aspirations Garden you will be given tools and techniques to help you come out of your comfort zone and experience the exhilaration of success and achievement until your subconscious mind will assume that your exciting new life of reward and success is actually your new comfort zone.

STEPPING OUT OF YOUR COMFORT ZONE

It is important that you challenge yourself or else your life will be stagnant and stale. To enhance your life stepping out of your comfort zone is vital, nothing amazing happens when you are afraid of feeling uncomfortable. When I first stepped out of my comfort zone I felt so uncomfortable and ill at ease, however I knew in my heart of hearts that if I really desired to stretch and grow as a person, and create a better life for myself I had to move beyond it.

Fear is a normal emotion when moving out of your comfort zone it is our body's way of letting us know that we are in fact moving out of our natural zone.

No one is immune from fear. You may be afraid of failing, being alone, off change or you may even feel afraid of doing something different to perhaps what your family and friends assume is the norm. It is imperative that you face your fears head on and continue to move past your current limits, you will find that bit by bit it becomes a little easier each time you continue to do so.

The Dreams and Aspiration Garden will gently coax you out of your comfort zone allowing you to release old outdated thoughts. If your thoughts are unproductive or negative, you will continue to experience the same reality, day in, day out! The Dreams and Aspiration Garden will help you to dream big and turn your dreams into your reality. You will awaken and pursue your Dreams and Aspirations in life with the tools and techniques of this amazing Garden.

The Garden of Dreams and Aspiration assists in breaking the habitual habit of your comfortable comfort zone. We have so many habits that are negative and remember that these habits in fact restrict your growth. It is an amazing feeling to break a habit, you will not acquire different results without doing something completely different to your normal default ways.

When I feel that I am slipping into my comfort zone, I make an effort to not allow myself to slip back into it by doing something different.

CREATING YOUR OWN HEALTH, WEALTH AND PROSPERITY

Discovering your potentiality to create health, wealth, prosperity and peace, is not only easy, it's also very exciting! You have the power within you to create anything in your life; this applies to good or not so good. In the Dreams and Aspirations Garden you discover that you had this power within you all along, it was merely buried deep within you along with those old outworn beliefs.

Would you like to discover perfect health and wellbeing?

You will find that The Garden of Dreams and Aspirations is the perfect way to develop an awareness constantly centred in health, wealth, prosperity and peace. When you are in this Garden you lift the veil of happiness and integrity, from your innermost being, resulting in your heart swelling with gratitude.

I have taken many of my clients on the journey of The Dreams and Aspirations Garden many times and have shown them how simple it is to step through the door of this garden.

Invariably my clients enter with a fearful chaotic mind but after several visits to this garden they generate peace to their very core. They experience their own being, just as you will, with an amazingly positive and constructive mind, from the influences of The Garden, empowering you to realise that you can have and live the life of your dreams.

Expectation is a powerful force and can influence how you live your life. Having high expectations rewards you with excellent results. In the Dreams and Aspirations Garden you are coached to have high expectations that award you with high performance, positive relationships and high achievements in all aspects of your life. Expecting the best means you are on the road to your Dreams and Aspirations. The Dreams and Aspiration Garden encourages making plans and expecting that those plans come into fruition by having great positive expectations.

> **If you put yourself in a position where you have to stretch outside your comfort zone, then you are forced to expand your consciousness.**
> Les Brown

A dream is your creative vision for your life in the future. You must break out of your current comfort zone and become comfortable with the unfamiliar and the unknown.
Denis Waitley

EXERCISE

Find somewhere where you can sit upright for 5 minutes undisturbed.

Sit down with your spine straight.

Take off your shoes and undo any tight clothing.

Breathe in slowly on a count of 4, holding in for a count of 4
and exhale slowly on a count of 4. Repeat 4 times.

Relax... You will find that thoughts or images will come
into your mind when you first begin...
do not pay any attention to them...
Simply allow them to drift away...
Drift...
Drift...
Drift away...

Keeping your eyes closed at all times.
Imagine you are standing in front of a tall mirror
and you can see your reflection in the mirror.

Notice what you are wearing, how your hair looks
and the shoes on your feet.
Do you look tired and ready for some tender loving care?

Carry on looking in the mirror.
Now close your eyes.
When you open your eyes next you will see yourself 6 months from now
where all your Dreams and Aspirations have been delivered to you.
Your Dreams and Aspirations have all been delivered to you; every
single thing you wished for is now yours.

Generate in your tummy that feeling of joy and true excitement of how
great it feels, you are free, you have your desires, yippee!!!

Open your eyes and see yourself in the mirror.

You are smiling.

Your face looks relaxed and happy.

You are glowing with happiness.

Keeping that feeling of happiness and excitement!

Look very deeply into your eyes and say out loud still looking into your eyes with deep meaningful gratitude "I am grateful and blessed that my dreams are now mine forever, thank you" and repeat 7 times.

Smile.

Feel good and feel grateful.

When you feel ready very gently open your eyes and come back to reality.

This exercise is recommended on a daily basis and is one of the keys to achieving your Dreams and Aspirations.

Adopting this amazing exercise on a daily basis will bring about profound changes in your life; the more this exercise is repeated the more powerful are the results.

Once you accept this powerful exercise and recognise your ability to change your life through it, you will enjoy following it as the benefits are so rewarding and empowering.

The Dreams and Aspirations Garden...

Within The Dreams and Aspirations Garden
you will learn amongst other things how to...

❁

Be guided into making firm decisions within your mind
to what your Dreams and Aspirations truly are
and pledge firmly that you will achieve them

❁

Be guided to achieve the Dreams and Aspirations that
you are aiming towards with a positive mindset and true belief

❁

Turn your Dreams and Aspirations into a firm plan of action
breaking down each Dream and Aspiration
into manageable steps to achieve them

❁

Be excited with vast enthusiasm, courage and pride
as your creativity juices will be flowing beyond belief
because you will know that your Dreams and Aspirations
are definitely achievable!

❁

Become a co-creator with the powers of your subconscious
mind who is your faithful Dreams or Aspirations Genie.
You will discover the magic of his powers
to creating an amazing life

❁

Be coached in how to set high expectations for yourself
as expecting only the best is what brings your
Dreams and Aspirations into reality.

❁

Manifest your Dreams and Aspirations
by being a co-creator with your subconscious mind.
Develop clear vision of consistently focusing
upon your Dreams and Aspirations.

Grace Brown

THE ANGEL GARDEN

Relates to your Angelic realm.
This Garden will show you how to open the door
to communicating with The Angels;
enabling you to start on a magnificent
journey of enlightenment.

The golden moments in the stream of life rush past us
and we see nothing but sand;
the angels come to visit us,
and we only know them when they are gone.
George Elliot

Go into The Angel Garden and make the Angels your best ethereal friends, be moved by their beautiful energy.

Allow their wisdom and illumination to sow your dreams in your tapestry of life.

THE ANGEL GARDEN

> Angels are infinite and omnipresent offer them
> your infinite love and laughter always
>
> Grace Brown

What is The Angel Garden?

Would you like to be guided to create your own destiny? The destiny that you truly desire, The Angels if allowed by you will guide you true and straight.

The Angel Garden will show you how The Angels help you to discover your thought energy which comes from the essence of your core being; you will discover how The Angels will in turn help you to direct that thought energy to influence the life you truly wish for.

Every angel has its very own individual qualities and capacity and they operate by connecting energies between Source energy and each individual; helping and influencing that individual to take a certain path.

> Ask for your desire.
> Release and let go of all expectations of
> how your desire will be yours, it just will be.
> Trust in your beautiful Angels.
>
> Grace Brown

WOULD YOU LIKE TO DISCOVER YOUR DIVINE SPARK AND PURPOSE IN LIFE?

When visiting The Angel Garden you will find The Angels will help you to determine your influence as the co-creator of your life. The Angels help you to determine your life purpose and ways of living a purposeful life. The Angel Garden and Angels have the power to generate ways to release your divine spark and your true potential. My belief is that unlimited potential is infinite within us all.

THE ANGEL GARDEN AND INTENTIONS

As you will discover later in this book I discuss the importance of intentions. The Angel Garden directs you to achieving strong powerful intentions, filled with fire and passion. The Garden helps you in setting your intentions, by firstly helping you to identify what you feel passionately about within your heart and secondly giving you the tools and power to bring those intentions into manifestation.

THE ANGEL GARDEN AND THOUGHT ENERGY

The Angel Garden works with thought and information. The Angel Garden and The Angels allow you to process explicit information essential throughout the creative process. The Garden and The Angels will help you to plant your seedlings (your thought energy) and nurture and protect the seedlings that are your dreams and desires.

THE ANGEL GARDEN AND THE UNIVERSAL LAW OF MIRRORS

The Angel Garden helps you to understand 'The Universal Law of Mirrors' and how it affects your life greatly in both positive and negative ways. Have you heard your friends say 'I always end up going out with losers' or 'I am always broke' or you may hear one of your friends state 'he or she always has Money, I do not know how they do it', all of these examples are influenced by The Universal Law of Mirrors.

If you constantly state 'I always end up with losers' then The Angels take that literally and in conjunction with The Universe you will always end up with losers!

Likewise if you state 'I always have money' then guess what....., exactly The Angels and The Universe take this literally and ensure that this is so.

The old saying of 'what goes around comes around' is simply The Universal Law of Mirrors in action; when you hear people say about someone's good fortune 'well they really deserve it' it is simply The Universal Law of Mirrors in action.

The Angel Garden will show you how to work with The Angels and The Universe to ensure the only things that are mirrored back to you are positive. The Angel Garden will show you that nothing happens by chance in The Universe and everything that does happen is for a specific reason.

THE ANGEL GARDEN AND THE UNIVERSAL LAW OF ATTRACTION

The Angel Garden will show you how working with The Angels will assist you in attracting people and circumstances into your life that are desirable to you by working with your higher self. The Universal Law of Attraction is constant and unwavering and always reflects back to you whatever you have given out.

You have probably heard the phrases 'money goes to money' or 'he always lands on his feet' or 'if he fell into a steaming pile of dung, he would come up smelling of roses'? All of these terms are the result of The Law of Attraction and The Angels in action, and is known as reaping and sowing.

The Angel Garden will help you to work with The Angels to attract what you truly desire into your life, once you connect with The Angels you will have unlimited power to attract what you truly desire.

DID YOU KNOW THAT YOU HAVE YOUR OWN PERSONAL ANGELS?

Everyone has their own angels that are personal to you; they are constantly connected to you. You may or may not be aware of your angel's presence around you; however your angels are with you right now while you are reading these words.

The Angel Garden teaches you how to communicate with your personal angels by speaking directly with your angels asking questions and more importantly receiving answers, although sometimes not in the way you would imagine.

MY PERSONAL ANGEL EXPERIENCE

Several years ago now I had my first proof that our Angels exist and are present with us at all times, 24/7. I had enrolled on a 3 year angel course, approximately 6 months into the course my tutor Anne, asked me if I had experienced my angels, I said that I hadn't but I was not concerned as I truly believed in Angels and did not need proof.

Anne my tutor expressed surprise as she explained the angels love to give you proof and it was about time that I not only believed but believed it with my own eyes. She told me, before going to sleep that evening to write in my journal that I would love to see the angels in action, and feel this with passion deep in my core while I was writing it. Just before going to sleep I offered thanks for my seeing the angels at work, I then dozed off to sleep.

I was awoken to such immense light I could barely open by eyes as the light was so strong it was blinding. I began to see through squinted eyes large poles of bluish white light being directed into my partner's body. There was a presence in this room I had never experienced before, it was truly astounding the feeling, colours and love that was present in that room.

I did not move I just sat upright in amazement, for how long I have no idea. I watched in wonder at the amazing rays of light that seemed to be penetrating my partner's body. I was not scared or frightened for what the angels were doing; I knew it was good because they only ever do things that are good. I was agog with what I was witnessing; it was truly spectacular watching them doing their work.

Suddenly it all went dark. They were gone or as my tutor later told me had actually finished healing my partner as he slept. I was sitting there in wonderment or was I dreaming or was I just in the most heavenly place ever. I knew if I was dreaming I would not be able to get up to make a cup of tea. I arose and made a cup of tea, came back to bed and left the cup on the bedside table and went to sleep.

I awoke the next morning wondering if it had all really happened or was it a dream. I noticed the tea cup and smiled, I knew it was not a dream. I had witnessed the most amazing thing ever. When I got up to have a shower right in front of the door was an enormous white feather; The Angels had left the feather as their calling card.

The Love of The Angel Garden and The Angelic Realm

On entering The Angel Garden you will find there are no right or wrong methods to communicate with your angel. But, The Angel Garden will show you that you have to accept yourself for who you really are, warts and all with all your faults and failures, with the all-encompassing compassion that you have within you. In return The Angels will offer you pure unconditional love. The Angels are extremely compassionate towards you, protecting you, never judging you and always hearing and responding to your requests for help.

Angel Support

Angels can offer more support in your life if you give them permission. I personally speak to my angels all of the time, I also send them Reiki healing, they love it and appreciate it so much I know because of the wonderful feeling that returns to me, simply beautiful.

As you become increasingly familiar with The Angel Garden and its Angels with the tools and techniques that work for you, you will find that you can contact your Angel whenever you wish.

If you are feeling unhappy or upset you will struggle to define the guidance that The Angels are offering you. Going into The Angel Garden helps you to become calm and clear, making it easier for you to perceive the guidance your angels are offering.

ANGEL VIBRATIONS

When your vibration is raised you are open to receiving clear direct guidance from your Angels. Having a higher vibration allows the Angels to transmit vital information so that your conscious mind accepts the information for manifestation to begin.

The Angel Garden helps you to raise your personal vibration, opening you up to different levels of consciousness and heightened awareness, developing your intuition in a conscious manner. Your increased awareness of energy develops your communication channels from various realms of spirit. Your reaction to your increased awareness of energy affects everything leading towards mental and emotional freedom.

ANGEL INTUITION

The Angel Garden helps in raising your vibratory rate so that you can recognise perceptions within you. The angels guide you to understand that your intuition comes from the core of your being. Your intuition is your instinct. It is your intuition that is your ability to perceive something as real and tangible.

The Angels Garden assists you in determining how you gather information for you to develop spiritually. You will awaken consciously listening more and more to your inner voice.

The Angels in the Angel Garden awaken you to your intuitive gift and teach you how to use your gift in an eclectic ways. You will learn how to distinguish not only your own emotions, also the emotions of others. You will use your intuition to gain clarity in any situation.

The Angel Garden can offer you the insight to your innate gift, incorporating your gift for your highest good and the highest good of others.

ANGELS AND AUTOMATIC WRITING

Everyone possesses the ability to hear the messages of love and guidance from the Angels. By visiting The Angel Garden, the love and guidance you receive through learning the method of automatic writing with The Angels will enrich you to your core essence.

Automatic writing is a technique that permits you to connect with your higher self and the Angels; you simply have to be guided through the process by the Angels themselves.

Through this method you gain insight about life areas that are significant to you at that particular moment in your life. Through The Angel Garden you will become acquainted with the beautiful Angels and realise how they will enhance your life for the better.

ANGELS AND CORD CUTTING

Cutting the cords of attachments is vital to sustaining good health and wellbeing and positive energy.

The cords are a form of attachment to people and situations. These attachments to people and situations are energy connections and remain enduringly entrenched in your energy system. In The Angel Garden the Angels show you how relationships carry these cord attachments, and how in some cases energetically they weaken your energy system because of the toxicity of the energy from certain toxic relationships and situations.

Not all attachments to energy are toxic, some are beautiful and loving; these are the ones that can remain as no damage will come from these. The toxic ones definitely need to be cut. The Angels will help you to discover how and what needs to be cut and perform a cord cutting ceremony to relieve you of the negativity that may be coming your way from these toxic relationships and situations.

SUMMONING YOUR ANGELS IN THE ANGEL GARDEN FOR THE MANIFESTATION OF YOUR DESIRES

In the Angel Garden you can summon the Angels to bring to you your true desires. Manifesting of your true desire will be set in motion once the Angels have been summoned and are aware of what the desires are. In The Angel Garden you will discover expansion and inner authenticity of who you really are and what you really wish for by working with the Angel Seed Map.

The Angel Garden will show you how to create your own seed map using pictures and images which will plant seeds that The Angels will help nurture until they are strong enough to be manifested as reality.

Eventually you will have an intrinsic understanding of what it is that makes a difference to you and what you really value in life.

ANGEL EXERCISE

If you have never worked with Angels before you will embrace how easy it is to work with the Angels receiving powerful, delicate and inspiring messages and guidance. Try this little exercise every day for thirty days to connect and create with the angels. This exercise is easy to do but will effectively change the way you live your life.

Firstly you will require:
A journal or notebook and a pen.
A white tea light candle (unscented) –
it helps to focus not only your energy but The Angels energy
Celestite Crystal - try and source a piece of raw Celestite crystal as this offers gentle uplifting vibrations and aids mental clarity.
Rose oil – this is a heavenly fragrance that transports you to the etheric realms of Angels and excellent when burned in an oil burner during your appointment with Angels.

Decide when you wish to meet with the Angels and write in your journal the date and time of your meeting. Let others in the home know that you do not wished to be disturbed for about 30 minutes.
Fifteen minutes before your appointment with your Angels burn the rose oil and light the candle.
When you feel ready sit down with your back upright.
Imagine that you have roots running from your feet into Mother Earth. Breathe in for a count of 4 and exhale for a count of 4. Repeat 7 times.

Imagine there is a ball of white energy approximately twelve inches above your head. Feel and sense this beautiful energy.
Imagine you are drawing energy from Mother Earth up the roots to the base of your feet, now from your feet up through your legs to the base of your spine. Continue up the spine to the throat and now to the crown (top of your head) imagining the Earth Energy shooting out of the crown of your head like a fountain.

The ball of white energy above your head begins to move into your crown, moving all of the way down to the base of the spine, down the legs and out of the feet into Mother Earth.

You are now grounded.

Angel Exercise Continued

Feel the warmth around you. Feel the beautiful peaceful energy.

To establish contact you must first invite the Angels in to your meeting. Greet them with warmth and a smile.

Write a question to your Angel in your journal.
The question can be anything at all.

Notice as you are breathing in the fragrance of rose oil you are drawing in the pure love of the Angels.

The answer to your question may be answered immediately or it could take time, the answer will come, trust it will.

After fifteen minutes or so ask your Angels to place their wings around you. Feel the Angels wings very gently fold around you embracing you with unconditional love. You are conscious of the closeness of the Angels and feel their love, beauty and forgiveness that touch the very depths of your being.

Stay like this until you feel that the Angels have given to you what you need at this point in your life.

Give thanks when you are ready and you feel that the Angels have departed.

Write a letter to the Angels in your journal; date it and state how they made you feel.

More than anything offer the Angels Gratitude; write down how grateful you feel.

Establishing contact with the Angels may not be successful with your first attempt, do not be discouraged. Communicating with the Angels takes time; allow patience to be your virtue.

Angel Beauty

Go into The Angel Garden and make the Angels your best ethereal friends, be moved by their beautiful energy. Allow their wisdom and illumination to sow your dreams in your tapestry of life.

All I can say from my very personal experiences is that the Angels not only enhanced my life, they have made my life a happier, plentiful, rewarding and magical one. Thank you Angels!

The Angel Garden...

**Within The Angel Garden
you will learn amongst other things how...**

The Angels will offer answers for you to achieve your desires

✺

**The Angels will determine ways of solving any dilemmas
or troubles you may be experiencing**

✺

**The Angels will offer to you assistance and direction to
whatever questions you may ask them**

✺

**The Angelic Realm opens the portal to many miracles
in your life**

✺

**The Angels show you how to become open and
receptive to Grace Energy in your life**

✺

**The Angels will offer assistance to develop
your career, family and relationships**

✺

Angels have no philosophy but love.
Terri Guillemets

THE FORGIVENESS GARDEN

Relates to you removing the shackles of un-forgiveness, enabling you to live a life of freedom and joy

Forgiving is rediscovering the shining path of peace that at first you thought others took away when they betrayed you.
Dodinsky

As you release, you will discover compassion and understanding, letting go of any umbrage towards the person that hurt you; just take that first step to complete forgiveness by walking into The Forgiveness Garden

THE FORGIVENESS GARDEN

> Resentment is like drinking poison
> and waiting for the other person to die.
> Carrie Fisher

The law of forgiveness is a very important law; it educates you to understand that forgiveness is an important key to how you live your life. The law of forgiveness brings closure, to release it completely, from your mind, body and spirit; releasing all of the emotion that you experienced at the time and letting it go.

> Always forgive your enemies - nothing annoys them so much.
> Oscar Wilde

If negative feelings are not released within you, illness may occur.

The key here is to understand that the suppressed feelings you have buried deep within you, can manifest into illness very quickly. Forgiveness is the key to how we progress in life! There will be no progression in your life without forgiveness in life!

> Forgiveness is a funny thing.
> It warms the heart and cools the sting.
> William Arthur Ward

CYCLE OF UN FORGIVENESS

The diagram below maps out the cycles of not forgiving and what manifests from not forgiving

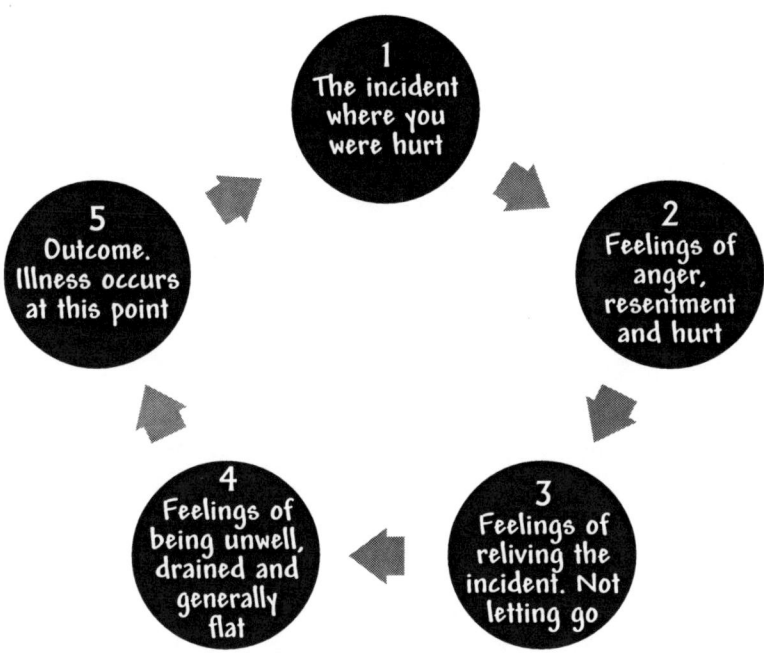

CYCLE OF UN FORGIVENESS

1. The incident occurs and you have feelings of humiliation and hurt. You are in a cocoon of hurt and pain, replaying the incident over and over again in your mind fuelled with pent up emotion. You feel the victim and are physically and emotionally encapsulated in a devaluing cycle that will destroy your quality of life.

2. The anger and pain that comes with the incident will have a massive affect on your whole life physically, mentally and emotionally. You will feel alone in your dilemma and afraid of dropping the barriers.

3. At this point of the cycle all the pain and anger is not only in your mind, it will be making itself at home in your body and your organs, maintaining negative and unproductive energy and holding onto the negative past event. At this point you are not thinking straight as your feelings of pain and hurt will be ingrained within you and part of your natural state of being.

4. It is at this point of the cycle that the stress from the upset you have been feeling has now manifested itself in your etheric layer of your subtle bodies. These manifestations will be toxic diseases, physical injury or physical trauma.

5. Physical illness occurs within the physical body and is a direct result of your unresolved emotional issue. The constant reliving and not releasing what has happened has given life to illness that is now expressed in the physical body. Illnesses can be in the form of high blood pressure, heart attack, ulcers, cold and in extreme cases cancer.

> FORGIVENESS IS LIKE FAITH. YOU HAVE TO KEEP REVIVING IT.
> Mason Cooley

CAN I BE FREE FROM THE HURT OF NOT FORGIVING?

Is there a way to be free from this emotion and can the devaluing cycle be stopped and released for you to live a happy, constructive, and healthy life?

Yes there is!

HOW TO BREAK THE UN FORGIVENESS CYCLE...

Forgiveness begins with you making the decision
to release what has happened

The forgiveness journey takes time and patience

Allow yourself the time to heal, try not rushing it.
Rome was not built in a day

In simple terms the concept of forgiveness has to be a strong one

Make a decision to embark on the journey of forgiveness

The end result is self-acceptance, freedom and purpose for living.

Go into The Forgiveness Garden and discover the unique tools and techniques for forgiveness.

Forgiveness comes more easily in the Forgiveness Garden because you are given faith, trust and security to move beyond the debilitating cycle of un-forgiveness.

It is the faith, trust and security of the Garden that enables to look beyond you. More importantly, it enables you to truly forgive.

HEALING YOUR MIND, BODY AND SPIRIT THROUGH FORGIVENESS

If you are suffering with not forgiving someone or something you will be hurting within and have emotions of anger, resentment, fear, sadness and many more traumatic emotions, which will be driving you crazy. In this state you are not hurting the wrongdoer; the only person being hurt is you. You are the only one who will be suffering for you not wishing to forgive.

Going into The Forgiveness Garden will be truly beneficial to your spiritual, mental and physical well-being. When you are unable to forgive it literally produces negative effects in all areas of your life, and therefore by going into the forgiveness garden you will discover how to release any negative judgements and learn to become more forgiving.

ARE YOU WILLING TO FORGIVE THE PERSON WHO HAS HURT YOU?

To forgive someone you have to be ready and willing to release and forgive. Only then will your life force energy begin to free flow easily

Embarking on the journey of forgiveness is your very own personal journey; there is no one else involved in the forgiveness process, only you

Forgiveness is acceptance. It is the acceptance of knowing the past is history and can never be revisited

Forgiveness is also acceptance that things can never go back to how things were

Forgiveness will heal deep emotional wounds, whether old or new

FORGIVENESS TABLE

See the table below for the pros and cons of forgiving and not forgiving.

Reasons for not Forgiving	Reasons to Forgive
I am giving in if I forgive	You will have closure to the situation
That person has one over on me	You can both move on in your lives
It means that person has got away with what they did	I am free from all the anger, hurt and resentment and I can heal
I feel bitter and twisted	Forgiving means I can feel gracious again
They will never be in my life again	You are free from constant thoughts about them, whether you see them again or not
If I forgive I am weak	I am a loving, caring person; I do not need to be hard and uncaring. By forgiving I show my true strength
They will be hurting the same way as I am, I want them to hurt	If I do not forgive I am the only one feeling the hurt and pain

Fill in your own personal forgiveness table below and see what the benefits are.

Reasons for not Forgiving	Reasons to Forgive

I am sure by filling in your own personal forgiveness table you already feel your mind, body and spirit being lifted into a better place. By taking these first steps to forgiveness you are showing your true maturity, strength and integrity which will only lead to a fabulous new life as you put the stressful parts of your past behind you.

RELEASE NEGATIVE JUDGEMENTS ABOUT YOURSELF OR OTHERS.

When you hold negative judgments about yourself and others you are not in a very good place and therefore forgiveness cannot flourish.

Only you can release the shackles of un-forgiveness, every feeling of resentment that you hold is like adding extra weight to a cart that you pull behind you in your everyday life.

The more resentment you feel the more weight you keep putting into that cart until it is such a burden to pull; it makes things for you increasingly difficult when travelling up and down the hills of everyday life than it should be.

Go into The Forgiveness Garden and begin to unload your cart and move on with your personal growth and development with renewed joy and energy.

CAN YOU TRULY FORGIVE?

Yes of course you can, I am not saying it is going to be easy though; The Forgiveness Garden is the first step on the path of forgiveness.

It offers you not only the wisdom to forgive and to understand what has gone on, it also gives you solid techniques to prevent the same mistakes from happening again.

EXERCISE

Make an appointment with yourself for a certain date and time.

If you have family ask if you can have some uninterrupted time on your own for about 45 minutes.

You will require a pen, paper and some envelopes (please do not worry you are not writing a letter to the people you are to forgive you are writing a letter to The Universe expressing your forgiveness).

Write down the name of everyone that you have a grievance with whether they are living or no longer with us.

Cast your mind right the way back to even your early school years. You will be astounded by the memories that come flooding back to you; you must be honest with yourself and list everybody who you think has wronged you for whatever reason.

If you need to forgive yourself for something that you wished you now had not done; then also write your name on the list.

Begin the process of forgiveness by writing the day and date at the top of the paper.

Write the following in an individual letter to each person. You may have to do this over several sessions before you have completed it.

You may feel reluctant or uncomfortable with the next step, forge ahead knowing that you will feel better for forgiving.

SAMPLE LETTER OF FORGIVENESS TO THE UNIVERSE

Date

Dear................

I am writing to you let you know I forgive you for whatever has gone on in the past.

I release and let go of you and surround you with light and blessings.

Go forth into the future with my unconditional blessings and enjoy peace in your life.

Please forgive me for not forgiving you sooner.

We are now both free to move on.

Blessings

Signed..

You will probably shed a few tears at the memories this brings; however you will feel release throughout your body which will feel amazing!

Now place your letter in the envelope and address it to:

> The Forgiveness Department
> The World
> The Universe
> UNI 1234

Seal it and put it to one side until you have finished the other letters; do not worry if your pile of envelopes is getting quite high as most of my clients end up with a skyscraper of a pile!

Now comes what I feel is the cleansing bit; take your envelopes outside and burn each letter (one at a time), holding each one with some kitchen tongues so that you do not burn yourself.

As you see the ashes of the paper release into the wind, take a deep breath in for a count of 4, hold your breath for a count of 4 and breathe out for a count of 4.

As you breathe out feel the freedom releasing, filling your body, feel your heart fill to the brim with gratitude for the forgiveness and releasing that has taken place.

> Forgiveness is the answer to the child's dream of a miracle by which what is broken is made whole again, what is soiled is made clean again.
> Dag Hammarskjold

The Forgiveness Garden...

Within The Forgiveness Garden
you will learn amongst other things how to...

Discover the tools to release the control and power the other person and situation has over you by offering true forgiveness

Discover faith, trust and security to move beyond the unbearable sequence of un-forgiveness

Learn how to work with the forgiveness wheel

Learn how to work with the magic of time. Time is a great healer and retreating into The Forgiveness Garden offers you magical positive outcomes you wish for and deserve

Learn how to not allow this to happen again in the future by making decisions in life to forgive instantly and take the relevant actions to forgive and create peace and space for good things in life to move in

When you decide that you wish to forgive you have to make a stronger commitment to yourself for a course of action for change.

Forgive.
It does not erase their crime but why should you do the time.
Let go of resentment.
Dodinsky

THE RELEASING AND LETTING GO GARDEN

Relates to you releasing and letting go of all negativity
from your mind, body and soul;
allowing you to live a healthy, happy and abundant life.

When you are angry, it is as if you a holding a burning coal.
Your anger is affecting only you and until you release it,
you will continue to do so.

The Buddha

In the Releasing and
Letting Go Garden
you can move beyond
the self-destructive
resentment that you feel.

In the Garden you are
free to release and let go
making your life
a happy and joyous one.

The Releasing and Letting Go Garden

Releasing and Letting Go is not always easy. Some people are very quick to forgive, not seeing any point in carrying the saga on, whereas others see only burnt bridges. Why is that? It is because there is a fundamental psychological difference between those who offer forgiveness readily and those who do not?

When you cannot forgive you are living in the past. The fact you are living in the past means that you are not present in this moment, it is the present moment "The Now" that is creating your future, so not only are you missing the important moment of NOW, you are creating a future connected to being unforgiving.

Please do not waste your time being in the 'NOW' by allowing your past to create your future; by not being prepared to release and let go of the negative parts of your past you cannot build the foundations for a positive future.

> **The stupid neither forgive nor forget; the naive forgive and forget; the wise forgive but do not forget.**
> Thomas S. Szasz

At a deep level, the subconscious mind is a collective consciousness of all the historical forms of perception positive and negative which exist throughout the physical body and subtle layers. By visiting The Release and Letting Go Garden you will be shown how to access this vital information stored within the subconscious mind and once located, how to release and let go all the negative history from your subconscious.

This negative history within your subconscious can lead to spiritual and psychological entanglements that then lead to suffering, resulting in illness of all types. The Releasing and Letting Go Garden will introduce to you tools and techniques that are used to remove those entanglements of suffering.

> **Forgiveness is a gift you give yourself.**
> Suzanne Somers

The Storehouse of Your Subconscious Mind

The dedicated use of The Releasing and Letting Go Garden will delve into the storehouse of your subconscious mind; any negative thoughts that are stored in the cellular memory of your organs and glands will be transformed into a storehouse of peace.

The Releasing and Letting go Garden teaches you how to not only release and let go but also allow prosperity, peace, health, wealth, and abundance to enter your mind, body and spirit. It is at this point in the Garden that the intentions offered with consciousness on a moment by moment basis will begin to influence what you attract into your life.

> When you hold resentment toward another,
> you are bound to that person or condition
> by an emotional link that is stronger than steel.
> Forgiveness is the only way to dissolve that link and get free.
> Catherine Ponder

Are You Holding On To The Past?

Your thoughts are constantly changing depending upon your frame of mind. To release and let go is imperative in resolving your feelings of hurt and anger as it is these emotions that stop you from forgiving. The resentment that you are feeling is not only a problem it is a self-destructive problem, it literally takes over your life.

In the Releasing and Letting Go Garden you can move beyond the self-destructive resentment that you feel. In the Garden you are free to release and let go making your life a happy and joyous one.

> Love is an act of endless forgiveness,
> a tender look which becomes a habit.
> Peter Ustinov

IS YOUR PAST STUCK TO YOU LIKE GLUE?

The Universal Garden of Release and Letting Go is an excellent place to be to let go of the past and understand, the past is history, it cannot be changed, it's gone. I know for many people, the past is like being shackled to a ball and chain; if this is you then your past will always be with you, and if you allow it, it can destroy your future.

The complex experiences that you have gone through in your life will be ingrained within you, sticking to you like glue. Those experiences will be good and bad, joyous and tragic. When you think about the good and joyous memories it lifts your soul and puts a smile on your face, good memories are great like a tonic.

Likewise, when you think about the bad and tragic memories these have a dramatic toxic effect on you; you feel empty, bitter and angry. It is these negative memories that have stuck to your subconscious mind like glue. If you allow these negative memories to overpower the good ones you will sooner than later become a slave to these memories with your whole being affected. But, there is light at the end of the tunnel for everybody, if you can start to tip the scales so that your memories are predominately good and joyous then you are sowing the seeds of a happy and healthy future; visit 'The Release and Letting Go Garden and be prepared to sow that seed of release and letting.

YOUR PAST WILL CREATE YOUR FUTURE IF YOU ALLOW IT TO.

The Garden of Releasing and Letting Go will help you to release people and situations from your past. Releasing and Letting go is therefore essential if you are to move on in your life successfully.

The garden offers tools and techniques to stop your past creating your future. In the garden you will discover ways to move beyond your self-defeating behaviours and change how you think and feel, touching base with your strengths and values.

A transformation occurs whilst you are in the Garden; you are creating your own reality as opposed to allowing circumstances to rule over you. You discover your personal power within you to create a new reality for yourself. You will move from living a restrictive life to living an empowering and exciting one.

Do You Feel Stuck In Life?

Strong negative emotions or trauma literally change your life force energy. Your energy becomes stuck, with the toxic emotions causing you to experience energetic congestion. This energetic congestion will manifest as pain or disease within your physical body resulting in tension, headaches, aches, pains and worse, stopping you leading a happy and healthy life.

Visiting The Releasing and Letting Go garden and discovering how to live in the present moment is important; The Garden offers you grounding and knowledge that you will not make the same mistake again.

> **The secret of forgiving everything is to understand nothing**
> George Bernard Shaw

Your Journey To Freedonia

The journey to Freedonia (freedom) is amazing. Your mind, body and spirit will develop, deepen and expand, plunging into the soul of cosmic reality. It is on this journey, that your mind discovers and understands that all things on this planet have a vibration. Knowledge is power, each thought is a vibration, and you have the power within you to change the vibrations around you to highly positive and powerful ones, changing your life for the better

The Garden of Releasing and Letting Go assists in removing the causes that have accumulated those effects that you have experienced previously so that you are released from the shackles from those effects. You move into another dimension of consciousness in the Garden where your Vibrational thoughts create reality.

> **Forgiveness is the key to action and freedom.**
> Hannah Arendt

Releasing Outdated Relationships

In 'The Garden of Releasing and Letting Go' whatever injustice you suffered in the past, you will be able to release it and let it go, giving yourself the freedom to move ahead in life.

When a friendship or relationship is formed there is an attachment of trust and loyalty between close friends or partners. It is in these relationships that we open up and share our innermost secrets with the people we trust.

These people offer refuge to tell all. We eventually bare our soul. When this person then goes on to betray us or greatly upset us in some way; it hurts us so deep into the core of our very being. The bond of trust has been broken, as we have bared our body and soul to this person so the wound inflicted on us by their betrayal is long and deep.

At the time of any betrayal, we may feel, bitter, angry, humiliated or all three. We will probably have questioned how can we go on, we may start to blame ourselves. At this low ebb in our life there is a bright light of healing waiting to shine upon us; resulting in our future being much happier and healthier than we could have ever imagined. That amazing healing light will only be turned on once we have decided to release and let go of what has happened to us in the past; then, and only then will our life begin to heal and move on for the better.

> **Forgiveness does not change the past, but it does enlarge the future.**
> Paul Boese

The tools and techniques in the Garden of Releasing and Letting go will empower you beyond belief. Offering forgiveness may not repair the closeness that you previously enjoyed, as there may have been too much water pass under the bridge. Releasing and letting go will restore faith in you to be bigger than the conflict. By having the humility to rise above a situation and deciding to release and letting go of resentment, judgment and pain; you will be at the same time embracing love, compassion and freedom.

EXERCISE TO RELEASE AND LET GO

Firstly, bring to mind what it is you cannot release and let go of.
Now you have brought to mind your problem how does it make you feel?
What word defines how you feel?

Become aware of the feeling and any sensations as you focus on them.
This may make you feel uncomfortable however it is an important part
of the exercise.

Feel how you are truly feeling right through your entire mind, body
and soul. If the feeling you are experiencing is one of pure sadness,
then cry, just cry and let it go. If your feeling is one of resentment,
you may feel as though you would like to blow your top,
jump up and down and shout if you wish.

Fully experience this feeling and understand that is all it is a feeling,
nothing more than that.

You now know it is just a feeling so release it by pressing
the thumb and first finger together and let it go.

Now say "I am ready to release and let go of this feeling now"
and FEEL the releasing and letting go and how good it feels
releasing all the obstructed energy that has been
stored in your mind, body and soul.
You will suddenly become aware of the tension diminishing,
feeling calmer and at peace.

You must persevere with this exercise as when feelings
have been stored for a long time it may take
several attempts to dislodge those feelings.

Understand, that the most important thing is you have to
recognise your negative emotions,
once you have recognised these negative emotions and feelings
then you can begin to release and let go as in the exercise;
if you do not recognise these emotions they will continue to happen.

The Release and Letting Go Garden...

Within The Release and Letting Go Garden
you will learn amongst other things how to...

Release and let go of negative feelings allowing you to move
forward in life without the baggage that holds you back

Release and let go the feelings of hurt and anger
that stop you from forgiving

When you do not release and let go you encounter unproductive
and self-destructive feelings that literally take over your life

By releasing and letting go a transformation within your mind,
body and spirit occurs; you feel free and finally at peace

Understand a feeling is just a feeling that needs
to be felt and released.

Releasing and letting go will restore faith in you
to be bigger than the conflict

Forgiveness is the final form of love.
Reinhold Niebuhr

THE FOUNTAIN OF YOUTH GARDEN

Relates to you transforming your mind, body and spirit by rejuvenating your energy on all levels. In this garden you will learn how to enhance your youthfulness and revive your spiritual essence.

There is a fountain of youth;
it is your mind, your talents, the creativity you bring
in your life and the lives of people you love.
Sophia Loren

The Fountain of Youth
Garden will help you to
develop enthusiasm
about who you really are.

You will gain faith and
assurance in how you look
and feel, building your
mind, body and spirit
to remain young at heart,
be young and
live a very long time.

Your new found
youthfulness will bring to
you much happiness
and confidence.

THE FOUNTAIN OF YOUTH GARDEN

> *The secret to staying youthful is to live honestly,*
> *eat slowly and lie about your age.*
> Lucille Ball

Would you like to hold off old Father Time a little bit longer?

Time waits for no one, tick-tock-tick-tock. Time is constantly ticking away for us all moment by moment, do not allow time to simply tick-tock by, take action and reap the benefits in all aspects of your life.

If you took heed of the media, TV and magazines, once you hit 30 it's a downward slippery slope, trying to hang onto your youth, grappling to discover the magic of staying young. Every day we see barrages of images of what is surmised as beautiful and it invariably is an image of a twenty year old model.

The general obsession regarding holding back old father time means that people are eager to part with huge amounts of money on anti aging products and cosmetic surgery to give the impression of being and feeling younger.

To look great and feel younger does not mean that you have to re-mortgage you home to look good. The Fountain of Youth Garden offers simple techniques and information to hold back old father time.

> *It is better to be beautiful than to be good.*
> *But... it is better to be good than to be ugly.*
> Oscar Wilde

RECLAIMING YOUR PERSONAL POWER, SPIRIT AND JOY

The Fountain of Youth Garden enhances your mind, body and spirit.

The Fountain of Youth Garden goes deep into the heart, to the root place and the essence of who you truly are, to reclaim your personal power, spirit, and joy.

The Fountain of Youth Garden restores, maintains and enhances your mind, body and spirit. It offers you new found passion and purpose, keeping your mind, body and spirit healthy and in balance.

> **The most beautiful thing we can experience is the mysterious. It is the source of all true art and science.**
> Albert Einstein

WOULD YOU LIKE TO ENCOURAGE WELLBEING AND VITALITY?

Simply because you are becoming mature does not mean that you have to decline in your physical and mental health.

It is perfectly possible to extend and improve good health as you grow older.

The Fountain of Youth Garden is a place that will enable you to encourage wellbeing and vitality, develop clarity within your mind and increase youthful appearance.

This life changing garden offers everything you need to stay young and in tip top condition for years ahead.

> **Solitude is painful when one is young, but delightful when one is more mature.**
> Albert Einstein

HOLDING BACK THE YEARS

You are a co-creator with your subconscious mind, you are what you think you are, you are what you perceive yourself to be; effectively holding back the years begins with the subconscious mind.

Your mind has amazing control over your body. Believing is not only achieving, it is a powerful medicine to alter physical symptoms. Expectation is a powerful force.

Change your mind, change your life. Put your mind to holding back old father time, the more you believe you are holding back the years will result simply in looking and feeling more youthful.

"You are as old as you think you are" If you think and feel old then old you will be. The Fountain of Youth Garden uses tools and techniques for clearing the hard drive of un-productive conditioning. The techniques of this Garden will give you the freedom to choose and maintain your most resourceful states.

Ivan Pavlov was a noted Russian physiologist who went on to win the 1904 Nobel Prize for his work studying digestive processes. Whilst Pavlov was studying digestion in dogs he noticed an interesting occurrence, each time the dogs were fed he would ring a bell; the dogs would begin to salivate as they were fed.

But, he found that if he rang the bell and did not feed the dogs they would still salivate. The dogs had been conditioned with the daily routine of feeding time, they simply associated the sound of the bell with food and by hearing the bell they subconsciously began to salivate.

This behavioural system affects many things in your everyday life. YOU ARE CONDITIONED. In The Fountain of Youth Garden the specific techniques on offer will greatly affect your mental and emotional state and how you think.

The Fountain of Youth Garden will enhance your thought processing which affects your emotional state, posture, thoughts and mind-set, while removing any negative limiting thoughts that you may have about yourself.

EXERCISE

Living in the present moment means that you are conscious of what is happening to you; you know what you are thinking, feeling and doing in that present moment. The present very soon becomes the past, meaning when that moment has gone, it has gone, it is history and cannot be changed.

It is being conscious of your thoughts, feelings and what you are doing that are vital for staying younger. The following table asks you questions about certain things that you do without really thinking about it. You do not think about them because they are habits that are formed within the subconscious mind, however they are habits that can be changed.

Please answer honestly.

Do you engage in any of the following?	Yes Regularly	Yes Sometimes	No Never
Do you smoke?			
Do you drink alcohol?			
Do you sleep well?			
Do you take recreational drugs?			
Do you use sunbeds?			
Do you spend excessive time in an air conditioned room?			
Do you take care of your skin?			
Do you drink water daily?			

There are two out of the eight that you should definitely have answered with a yes - regularly and everyone should be doing them every day, men and women; can you guess which they are?

The water is one of them and the other is taking care of your skin and it is these two things along with how you think that affect your youthfulness.

You will discover in The Fountain of Youth Garden that drinking water is vital for your body to function correctly and keep your skin plumped up; men should drink 3 litres a day and women 2 litres.

Taking care of your skin along with exercise and proper sleep will definitely hold back old father time and delay the natural aging process.

Concerning the other questions that you may have answered yes to, these greatly affect your health and well being and are not good for you. By going into The Fountain of Youth Garden you will discover how to use the youth seed map, youth journal and other techniques to hold back old father time, and start to turn back some of the affects these bad habits have caused.

> **One problem with gazing too frequently into the past is that we may turn around to find the future has run out on us.**
> Michael Cibenko

THE AFFECTS OF THESE BAD HABITS INCLUDE

Alcohol

Drinking alcohol and the aging process are related in many ways. Alcohol lowers your calcium levels and impedes your body's capacity to absorb calcium; this means if you are a heavy drinker you will be at risk of brittle bones and other deficiency problems.

Smoking

If you are a smoker of many years you will have lines or wrinkles on your face, classically around the mouth and the corners of your eyes and possibly have quite deep lines on your cheeks and around your lower jaw. If you are relatively young these ageing signs will not yet be apparent, however they will be developing with each puff of your cigarette.

Drugs

If you do take any form of recreational drug then The Fountain of Youth Garden is for you as it is in this Garden where habits can be changed and replaced with new positive healthy ones.

Sun beds

Sun beds as proof suggests causes premature ageing of the skin. Being on sun beds means your skin becomes rubbery, tough and wrinkled from a young age. So when your tan fades, the damage is already done.

Pollution

Air pollutants are damaging to the skin due to restricted flow of oxygen and nutrients to your skin, your pores become blocked, it is essential that you implement a regular skin care routine to combat these effects.

Sleep

Sleeping well will take you a step closer to flawless skin. Sleeping well gives your skin the boost required to rejuvenate itself. When you sleep the restorative process begins. In The Fountain of Youth Garden tools and techniques are available to aid in you enjoying rejuvenating sleep.

Do you think that you take care of yourself?

Taking good care of yourself is essential for you to preserve balance of mind, body and spirit. In The Fountain of Youth Garden you learn about longevity and slowing down the ageing process.

Age related illnesses and diseases that occur should not be considered to be a predictable part of getting older; it should be thought of that prevention is better than cure. It is vital that you take action, to take responsibility for yourself now.

I have memories –
but only a fool stores his past in the future.
David Gerrold

WOULD YOU LIKE TO REPAIR YOUR MIND BODY AND SPIRIT?

The Fountain of Youth garden encapsulates repairing your body, igniting your passion physically, emotionally and spiritually. It provides access to incandescent meditation, healing energy and bodily wisdom. The Fountain of Youth Garden empowers you by placing the skills you require for healing, bringing to you peace and vitality, joy and health in abundance.

> **Live, laugh and love yourself to greater health, wealth, and prosperity, whilst holding back old father time.**
> Grace Brown

The Fountain of Youth Garden...

Within The Fountain of Youth Garden
you will learn amongst other things how to...

Live a healthy and optimistic lifestyle, giving you a longer life
and greater well-being

Aspire to live a healthy, balanced life

Think, live and breathe health in your body, in your mind, in
your finances and in your relationships

Discover the real you as a splendid, unique being with
boundless potential and aptitude for experiencing the beauty
and love of yourself and extending love to others

View the world in all of its full shining glory and live, laugh
love with gushing youthful energy

Understand the highest importance of power of the
subconscious mind and consciously fuel it with positive thoughts

Understand that having an optimistic attitude to change
decreases the progression of physical ageing in the body

Understand that the power of your subconscious mind
increases the strength of your will power

Understand when your mind is strong, your body will be strong

Keep your interest in life at a maximum level by surrounding yourself with the company of passionate and optimistic people. You will in turn be injected with enthusiasm by their positive attitude.

Grace Brown

THE CRYSTAL GARDEN

Relates to you bringing harmony to your mind,
body and spirit through the use of crystals.
Working on the subtle layers and chakras
you will discover your connection to Mother Earth;
learning to channel unwanted energies
back to her for recycling.

Once you have discovered the unique energies of your beautiful crystals; these energies will not only harmonise and rebalance all aspects of your life, but will draw to you people, events and circumstances that you truly desire.

All you have to do is take that first step into The Crystal Garden.

THE CRYSTAL GARDEN

Would you like to accelerate your personal well-being with crystals and gem stones?

Taking the path into The Crystal Garden is an amazing journey to accelerating your personal and spiritual growth, increasing your faith and making strong, supportive, spiritual connections.

The Crystal Garden is a beautiful place that nurtures that inner part of you that yearns to understand who you really are, what your life purpose is and why you are here. More importantly, it enables you to release your full potentiality, making you more in control of manifesting your personal truth.

The potent healing properties of The Crystal Garden is amazing, the Crystal Garden experience provides a personalised, practical and direct experience of how crystals can heal your life. On your journey you will be taken deep into the heart of yourself, developing your ability in visualisation and intuition.

> **We must first know the self before studying the universe.**
> Richard Rose

THE CRYSTAL GARDEN OF INFINITE POSSIBILITIES

The Crystal Garden will enable you to step through the doorway to infinite possibilities, finally removing the barriers that have held you back from achieving your goals.

Stepping into the garden offers you a series of practical tools and exercises that will help you to create success in your life; develop your intuition and fulfil your unlimited potential.

You will learn how to flow with the Universe, become a conscious co-creator in this amazing Universe, a practical mystic and passionate manifester.

> **Only those who believe there is a path will ever find one.**
> Richard Rose

YOUR HEALTH IS IN YOUR HANDS.

It is important that you take responsibility for your physical and emotional health; The Crystal Garden brings to light when and why you are not practicing self care.

Not taking care of you means that physically and emotionally you will be challenged. Little things in life that you normally would shake off will start to bother you; your energy levels may drop; all in all you will feel wiped out.

The Crystal Garden offers terrific tools and techniques of self care; I have witnessed many clients applying The Crystal Garden techniques in their lives and they have flourished beyond belief.

All our emotions and thoughts are conditioned reflexes, reactions.
Vimala Thakar

Your Energy and the Crystal Garden

When I drive my car I am using fuel; when the fuel begins to run low I refill up my car with fuel. If I do not then the car will stop; your body is no different to a car.

You body is your vehicle through life. You cannot run on empty, you have to refuel your body. We all do this by making sure we have enough sleep and exercise, as well eating the right type of food. All of these can be greatly enhanced by relaxing in The Crystal Garden for at least once a day for 30 days.

By making a concerted effort to take care of your mind, body and spirit; maintaining good positive habits, as well as keeping your energy tank topped up, you are able to gain control over your life.

Taking care of you is doing what feels right to you; see yourself as a unique being with many gifts and talents; look deep within you and watch yourself grow as a person.

> Rekindle the joy yachtsman that lies deep inside of you;
> share magic crystals and watch it grow!
>
> Isabel Yosito

HOW THE CRYSTAL GARDEN WILL ENHANCE MIND, BODY AND SPIRIT

By controlling your mind, you become the master of your very own Universe.

Your mind, body and spirit love creativity, conscious awareness and well-being. Being in the Crystal Garden your mind, body and spirit will be healed, balanced and awakened to everything the Universe has to offer you.

The Crystal Garden will encourage your mind to be active, open and receptive to learning new skills. The Crystal Garden offers you adequate peace and harmony restoring your mind, body and spirit to enjoy enhanced well-being. Your spirit will be restored in The Crystal Garden, building your faith and discovering your purpose in life.

Everything in your life relies on your spirit being strong. The Crystal Garden offers you support in strengthening your spirit, a strengthened spirit enhances all areas of your life.

In The Crystal Garden you can focus on feeling gratitude, unconditional love and compassion for you and others, bringing your emotions as well as your mind, body and spirit into balance.

The imagination imitates. It is the critical spirit that creates.
Oscar Wilde

UNLOCKING YOUR DEEPEST INTENTIONS WITH CRYSTALS AND GEM STONES

In The Crystal Garden you will discover the magical journey of insights and awareness which will bring you the keys to your own truths. Unlocking your deepest intentions, personal inspiration, creative energy and passion as your explore the amazing Crystal Garden.

Working with stones and gems will enhance a feeling of well being, spirituality and discover who you really are and what you truly desire.

You can discover your own affinity to crystals.

I use crystals daily for their beautiful energy. I simply love them and have such an affinity with them. I have found myself drawn to some of the strangest looking ones, however when I touch them, I know why, it is the beautiful energy that they offer to me.

I have a large piece of rose quartz that is raw and is the size of a large piece of coal, it is adorable. I sit with it on my lap and feel the beautiful healing energy that it gives me.

Using crystals will awaken your heart chakra to your gut instincts, your love and compassion, your consciousness thereby guiding you to make the right choices in any given situation. You will grow on your journey to enlightenment with love, joy and optimism.

You will discover how other crystals can enhance your life in the Crystal Garden

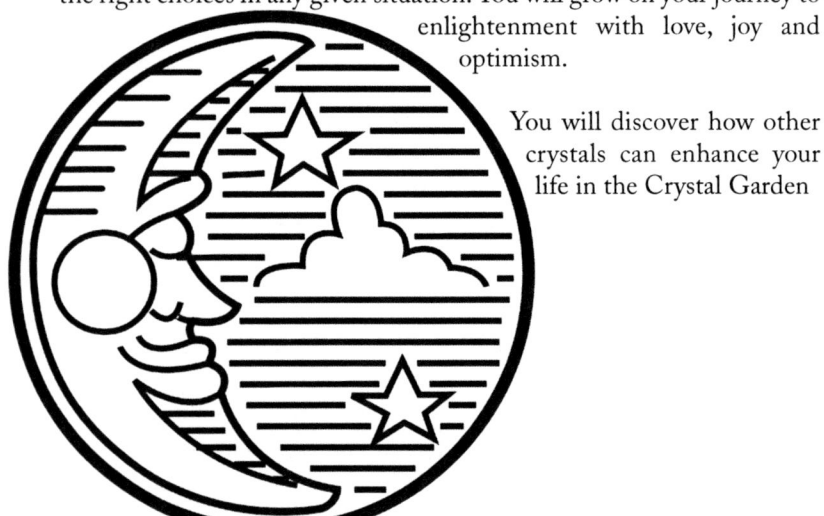

SOME OF THE QUALITIES OF ROSE QUARTZ...

Rose quartz is a master healer

Rose quartz is fantastic for removing negativity and helps to promote a calm ambience around the home; I have chunks of it in each room.

Rose quartz is said to be the stone of unconditional love

Rose quartz invites love to come to people who struggle to discover love within them and also giving love to others

It will enhance any meditation or quiet time as it is a harmoniser and balancer of energy

When there is emotional upheaval, chaos, disturbance or unease rose quartz is brilliant for soothing the heart chakra after such given situations

It helps to open and re-balance the heart chakra thereby showing great compassion

Rose quartz is a stone of friendship

It promotes self esteem

Rose Quartz enhances love for oneself and others

Rose Quartz has healing properties, especially comforting for burns

It protects you from electromagnetic emissions. So, if you work with a computer regularly then place a piece of rose quartz next to your computer.

Did you know that good things come in small packages?

Determining the right crystal for you need not be difficult. do not make the size a big thing or how beautiful it is; remember great things come in small packages. I have a simply amazing stone that looks boring and quite dull; however the energy it emits to me is really something else, I adore working with that stone.

Be aware that when working with raw stones their natural shape and state may not be too attractive; however they are as potent and actively powerful as their polished and cut equivalents.

Did you know that stones are personal to each individual?

When buying your stones it is important that you make sure that it is the correct crystals for you.

It is best if you can hold the stone, therefore getting a good feel for the stone.

If you feel that a particular stone that you have handled does not feel right for you, then that is not the stone for you so place it back.

Stones are very personal to each individual and if they do not feel right now then they certainly will not feel right when you are performing your exercises.

I do have some of the funniest looking stones because as I stated before the prettiest are not always right for you, and you are not right for every crystal. You see the relationship between you and your crystal has to be right for both of you and not one way.

> Emotion arises at the place where mind and body meet.
> It is the body's reaction to your mind or
> you might say a reflection of your mind in the body.
> Eckhart Tolle

WHICH IS THE RIGHT STONE FOR YOU?

This is a very simple way of knowing if the stone is right for you or not, hold the stone in your dominant hand (if you are right handed then hold the stone in your right hand) for several moments, feel the energy, sense if it feels right to you, you will know when it is right.

You may find that certain crystals will feel sticky as though they are energetically stuck to your fingers. Others will make you feel joyous; if this happens to you then you have indeed found your crystal.

If you and a stone are not meant to be together, you will have a sense of hesitation that will be especially evident; this stone is not meant for you, it is for someone else.

Simply keep choosing until you find the stone that is meant for you.

HOW TO FIND THE RIGHT STONE...

Hold the crystal in your dominant hand.

Now offer the stone gratitude for helping you;
this opens you up to receive the crystal energy.

Breathe in slowly and deeply, throughout the whole process.

Look at your stone, move it around in your hand.

Take notice of any bursts of light and rainbows.

Focus on the colour of the stone.

If any of your stones are clear, simply focus on white light.

Feel the shape of your crystal.

Feel the texture of your crystal.

Move the crystal over your fingers and rub it with your thumb.

Hold the crystal in the palm of your hand, as this is your palm chakra
it will help you to not only feel your crystal,
it will help you to also feel its energy.

When you are tuning into your crystal, perceive if you are aware
of any other vibrations with in different parts of your body.

If you feel that you are drawn to keeping hold of the crystal,
try holding it next to your heart chakra; perceive any sensations,
imagery, or thoughts that come into your mind.

If you really do not feel anything at all then that
particular crystal is not for you.

CRYSTALS AND CHAKRAS

Below is a table of the seven stones we will be using in The Crystal Garden.

It is entirely up to you whether you buy them all or maybe one or two of them, they are fairly cheap to buy. I would definitely recommend that of all of them a piece of raw rose quartz is essential.

Stone	Colour	Meaning	Chakra
Garnet	Dark Red Burgundy	Self Esteem	Base
Carnelian	Dark Orange	Energy Booster	Sacral
Citrine	Yellow/White	Personal Power	Solar Plexus
Rose Quartz	Pink	Love	Heart
Blue Lace Agate	Powder Blue	Encourages Peace	Throat
Sodalite	Indigo	Peace and Happiness	Third Eye
Amethyst	Violet	Clears Energy Obstructions	Crown

The Crystal Garden...

Within The Crystal Garden
you will learn amongst other things...

How to connect with your crystals and attune them to your
mind becoming one with your consciousness

How to discover to combine various crystals for health,
wealth and abundance

A technique that will reinforce your connection to the earth
and convey a stronger flow of earth energies
that will enhance mind, body and spirit

How to combine your personal energy with that of
gem stones for self healing and self love

How to make a Crystal Manifesting Box to manifest
all that you wish for in life

How to make your personal Crystal Grid to
enhance all aspects of your life.

In the attitude of silence the soul finds the path in a clearer light, and what is elusive and deceptive resolves itself into crystal clearness. Our life is a long and arduous quest after Truth.
Mahatma Gandhi

THE GRATITUDE GARDEN

Relates to having or not having gratitude in your life.
It will show you how to be grateful for everyone
and everything in your life;
which then brings you more things to be grateful for.

It is very important to understand that whatever you offer with your words, thoughts or actions will ultimately return to you.

Everything that you give out in these ways is mirrored back to you.

THE GRATITUDE GARDEN

> Go into the gratitude garden and plant seeds
> of thankfulness for everything in your life,
> even if yours has been a roller coaster life.
>
> Grace Brown

What is Gratitude?

I have the attitude of gratitude in my everyday existence. I am grateful for everything in my life.

When I awaken I offer my thanks to my Angels and the Universe for my being here to live another wonderful day.

Gratitude is a state of BLESSEDNESS; anyone can achieve a state of BLESSEDNESS in The Gratitude Garden, making gratitude as your natural state of being.

We take so many things for granted in our everyday life; the fact that we have clean running water at our disposal anytime we desire, we just turn on the tap. We can have a shower, take a bath, wash our hair, make a cup of coffee and wash our clothes whenever we wish, however do you show Gratitude for this fact?

Have you ever stopped to show Gratitude for your body? All the wonderful things that your body does for you are astounding and yet so few show Gratitude for their life vehicle.

Daily Gratitude will bring about a positive state of mind. A positive state of mind will draw to you the people, circumstances and events that your heart desires.

GRATITUDE EXERCISE

Sit down somewhere quiet and close your eyes and feel the darkness.

Imagine how you would feel if your world was dark
due to not having any sight from your eyes.

Imagine what it would be like to go through your day to day life
in complete darkness.

Imagine never being able to see your loved ones,
not being able to do your job, not being able to drive,
not being able to enjoy your favourite hobby or pastime,
not being able to watch a film or see a beautiful view.

It does not bear thinking about does it?

Now, open your eyes slowly and look around you,
be grateful that you enjoy the most amazing thing that is sight;
be grateful that by having the gift of sight you are able
to do all the things that you previously may have taken for granted.

Make today the day that Gratitude becomes your Attitude to life.

> **When it comes to life the critical thing is whether you take things for granted or takes them with gratitude.**
> Gilbert Keith Chesterton

Go into The Gratitude Garden today and learn the art of being grateful.

DO YOU OFFER GRATITUDE DAILY?

You may be thinking, how can I feel gratitude when I am overwhelmed with various problems in my life. The Gratitude Garden is not merely a garden for discovering gratitude, it is your 'wake up and smell the roses' garden as well as a place of unlimited opportunities.

It is very important to understand that whatever you offer with your words, thoughts or actions will ultimately return to you. Everything that you give out in these ways is mirrored back to you.

You have all heard the phrases "you reap what you sew" and "what comes around goes around" or you may have heard "he/she had it coming" or "money goes to money".

These are all examples of the simple rule of mirroring; when you offer much gratitude, gratitude is returned back to you. When you offer someone kindness and compassion, then you receive kindness and compassion.

But on the other hand if you are unkind and uncharitable to people then guess what; you will receive unkind and uncharitable things in your life.

EXERCISE

EIGHT THINGS TO BE GRATEFUL FOR...

Take a look at the Gratitude Table

The first table is my personal table with 8 things
that I am grateful for listed.

In the blank table all you have to do is write 8 things
in your life that you are grateful for.

In the centre column it asks you what action
you are taking to demonstrate your gratitude.

The third column asks how frequently you show gratitude
for what you are grateful for.

MY PERSONAL GRATITUDE TABLE

What are you Grateful for?	What action are you taking to demonstrate your Gratitude?	How Frequent
I am grateful for my health	Writing my gratefulness in my journal and affirmations	Everyday
I am grateful for my family	I tell them everyday how much I love them and how grateful I am to have them in my life	Everyday
I am grateful for my friends	I tell my friends how they all enrich my life	Everyday
I am grateful for my compassion in life	I show compassion as often as I possibly can	Everyday
I am Grateful for my home and my possessions	I write in my journal and repeat affirmations of gratefulness	Several times a day
I am grateful for my finances and that I pay all my bills on time	I write in my journal and repeat affirmations of gratefulness	Several times a day
I am grateful for my car	I write in my journal and repeat affirmations of gratefulness	Several times a day
I am grateful for my career	I write in my journal and repeat affirmations of gratefulness	Several times a day

Most human beings have an almost infinite capacity for taking things for granted.

Aldous Huxley

YOUR PERSONAL GRATITUDE TABLE

What are you Grateful for?	What action are you taking to demonstrate your Gratitude?	How Frequent

This process must be done on a daily basis, although being compassionate and kind should be in your life at all times.

After 21 days you will start to see the magic happen, showing constant positive gratitude in your life for all things will result in you receiving and meeting positive people and situations.

MAKE GRATITUDE YOUR ATTITUDE

In the Gratitude Garden, you will discover that gratitude is an attitude and a great attribute in life. The garden techniques and tools guide you to becoming a conscious creator, taking control of your own life and future happiness!

> To think creatively, we must be able to look afresh at what we normally take for granted.
> George Kneller

DO YOU OFFER GRATITUDE FOR YOUR HEALTH, FRIENDS, AND FAMILY?

Some people do not appreciate what they have until it is gone. When I say gone, it could be health, wealth, love, loss of a family member, loved one or friend. We have no idea what is in store for us, people, circumstances, love, the list is endless.

The Gratitude Garden offers techniques for offering gratitude NOW, and embracing what you care about in your life now.

IS YOUR GLASS HALF FULL OR HALF EMPTY?

I can honestly say with my hand on my heart, that my life has had many ups and downs, has been colourful in many ways, and been blessed with the people that I have met on my life's path. However, gratitude has made the biggest impact on my life and for that I am immensely grateful!

In the Gratitude Garden you will discover tools for focusing your attention, and techniques for you to attract more of the things that you would love to enjoy, and can be grateful for.

You will discover in the Garden how to look at all aspects of your life as being a glass that is half full rather than a glass that is half empty.

> If a fellow isn't thankful for what he's got,
> he isn't likely to be thankful for what he's going to get.
> Frank A. Clark

The Gratitude Garden...

Within The Gratitude Garden
you will learn amongst other things...

How to discover your personal Gratitude Manifesting Box.
Your Gratitude Manifesting Box will draw to you
more things to be grateful for

'The Attitude of Gratitude' which will make a huge impact
on your life and well-being

How to achieve a state of pure unadulterated BLESSEDNESS
in The Gratitude Garden, making gratitude your
natural state of being

How discovering a grateful state of mind will draw to you
the people, circumstances and events that your heart desires.

How to plant Gratitude seeds on your
personal Gratitude seed map

How you will discover the silver chord, achieving
and receiving pure gratefulness in life.

Gratitude is an attitude for life;
it should be like a subconscious habit,
make it your habit.
Grace Brown

Conclusion

Healing not only yourself but also your life is a complex subject, delving very deep into the core of your being is what is required if you are to heal.

This book has given you diverse tools and techniques to heal all aspects of your life. Your healing is not just about one aspect of you it is about every aspect of you.

> Forgiveness is the economy of the heart...
> forgiveness saves the expense of anger,
> the cost of hatred, the waste of spirits.
> — Hannah More

The Money Garden offers amazing techniques to help you to drop any barriers you may have regarding money. You will learn how to attract money and equally important hold on to it.

The Love Garden is influential in helping you to create love in every aspect of your life from learning to love yourself as well as others. You will discover that love and true blessings in The Love Garden will transform your life beyond belief.

The Goals and Desires Garden offers tools and techniques help you set and complete your goals within the time frame you set. It will show you how to have the necessary confidence to change your life.

The Guardian Angel Garden will show you how to ask for a message, how to be open and receptive and to be able to hear and understand your Guardian Angel.

The Healing Garden shows you the mind, body and spirit connection to your health as well as how to release disrupted or stuck energy.

The Dreams and Aspirations Garden guides you into making firm decisions to what you truly desire and shows you how to pledge firmly that you will achieve them. It will guide you towards your goals and give your true belief.

The Angel Garden will offer answers to you to achieve your desires. It will allow your Angels to determine ways of solving any dilemmas or troubles you may be experiencing.

In The Forgiveness Garden you will discover the tools to release the control and power the other person and situation has over you by learning the path to true forgiveness.

The Releasing and Letting Go Garden will show you how to release outdated beliefs, let go of negative feelings and restore your faith in yourself, allowing you to be bigger than the conflict.

The Fountain of Youth Garden shows many ways of enhancing yourself, resulting in you feeling, looking and acting great!

The Crystal Garden will enhance your spirituality with not only the universe but within yourself.

The Gratitude Garden opens your eyes to be grateful for what you have in your life now; with this gratitude you will be releasing many further amazing things into your life.

YOUR JOURNEY STARTS HERE...

When healing begins to occur in one area, it becomes easier for further healing to occur in other areas of your life. It is important to realise healing your emotions is paramount, as we become what we think.

Your emotions are real and in some cases deadly. Emotions cannot be repressed because they can have a dangerous impact on your life. Emotions do not like to be repressed so the information in this book will help you to acknowledge, feel and release these emotions.

Having good intentions is of upmost importance in life as it is the intentions that fuel the words that matter. Make it your goal to be, do and have the best of intentions and learn to release and let go of whatever is not serving you well anymore with those best intentions.

Make The Pathfinder your best friend and reference book to healing your Mind, Body and Spirit; keep it close to you revisiting it on a regular basis.

Whichever Universal Garden you choose to go into will serve you well and bring about healing to your Mind, Body and Spirit.

The Universe wishes you to have your dreams and desires and is always guiding and directing you to where you are meant to be. Be directed by the Universe and show non-resistance in life, move into the flow and remain there happy and very grateful.

Enjoy

YOUR FREE GIFT...

As a token of our appreciation, we have provided all readers with a free Universal Gardens Pathfinder Workbook. You can download this for free at www.TheUniversalGardens.com.

The workbook contains blank copies of the Universal Garden Wheel as well as blank forms from the Pathfinder for you to print and use.

Also in the Universal Gardens Series...

This Pathfinder is your introduction to the Universal Gardens.

If you want to see what other books, journals and audio meditations are available, then take a look at our website.

www.TheUniversalGardens.com

 www.facebook.com/UniversalGardens

  www.twitter.com/ugbooks

 www.youtube.com/user/UniversalGardens

The Universal Gardens Daybook
(Available annually)

Make this your best year ever!

We lead such busy lives - it is easy to become disorganised in a sea of chaos. Here is the answer!

Use this DayBook to keep track of your goals, to create a journal of your year, to organise your time and to find inspiration.

Use this DayBook to keep track of your journey through each year! The DayBook will help you set out your goals and give you purpose to your year.

I bought this book for myself instead of buying the usual journal I buy every year. Well this is a journal with a difference, what a little gem! This is a beautiful book, full of inspirational quotes, stunning illustrations and wonderful tips for getting the most out of life. And if you're ever having a bad day, then a little look at this book is guaranteed to lift your sprits. There is plenty of space to write in daily, with the added bonus of the 'feel good' quotes and advice.
I would recommend this to anyone who wants to get motivated and organised.
Amazon Review

The Universal Gardens Journal

This unique and ground-breaking Journal is designed to help you track and change your life over six months.

In this journal you can observe, document and analyse your world as you explore the Universal Gardens.

But it is more than just a journal!

There are pages of useful instruction and guidance to help you break old habits and form new and powerful ways of living.

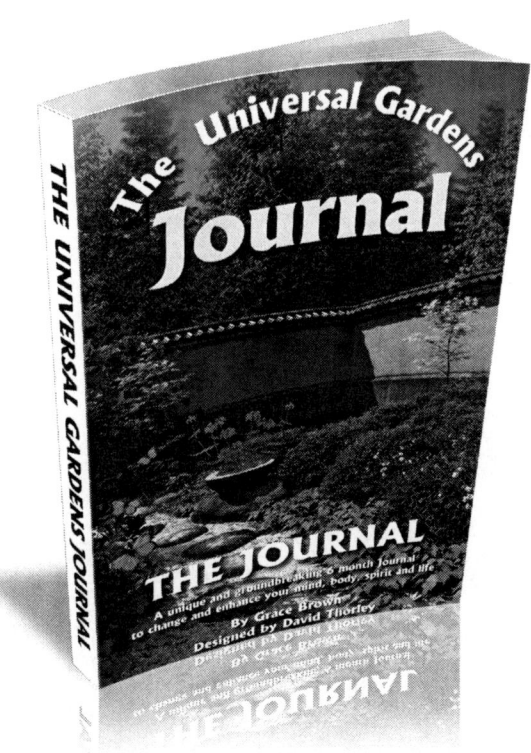

The Money Garden

In The Universal Garden of Money you will learn

How to find out how much money
you really need and when you need it

How to stop your money being frittered away

How to manifest even more money

How to visualise and manifest money

How to access 'The Universal Garden Bank' where you will have
a debit card with unlimited credit that is used
in the Universal Garden Bank's ATM

By deciding to enter the Universal Money Garden you are clearing a path that, if followed correctly, will bring you your dreams and desires in abundance.

As well as the handbook, the journal will allow you to chart your progress. Also available a CD read by Grace, taking you into the Money Garden whenever you want!

Handbook   CD   Journal

The Love Garden

Relates to the love of you, your spouse, family and friends.
If you are lacking in this area, this garden will help you to discover the golden thread of love.

Discover the golden thread of love within you.

Discover 'The Love Genie' with his lamp, for you to rub
and bring all your loving desires into being.

Begin liking and loving yourself.

Learn to attract the love of your life.

Plant your loving seeds in your personal seed map.

Discover your own mantra to attract true love.

Bathe in The Fountain of Love.

By deciding to move into 'The Universal Love Garden'
you are opening the doors to an amazing world of love,
enlightenment and true appreciation of true love in your life;
all you have to do is have the courage
to walk through that door.

Handbook   CD   Journal

The Goals and Desires Garden

Relates to you discovering what your true goals and desires are in life; as well as showing you how to achieve them.

How to set and complete your goals perfectly
in the time frame you set, with confidence,
and a great sense of accomplishment

How you will change your life by
learning how to change your mind

By setting sharp, clearly defined goals,
you'll see forward progress in what might previously
have seemed a long pointless grind

How setting goals will lift your self-confidence

How you will recognise your own skill and ability
in setting and achieving your goals

How you will discover the GOLDEN KEY
to goal setting and achieving your goals.

Handbook	CD	Journal

The Guardian Angel Garden

Relates to you discovering your personal Guardian Angel that has been with you on your journey from birth until your death.
This garden will help you to identify and make contact with your Angel; enhancing not only your life but your Guardian Angels too.

You will learn how to ask for a message

How to be open and receptive to
your question being answered

How to understand your Guardian Angel

You will learn how to communicate with your Guardian Angel

Establish regular contact with your Guardian Angel

Learn from your guardian angels

Handbook   **CD**   **Journal**

The Healing Garden

Relates to the health and well being of your life.
You will find that true healing occurs at source level in this garden.

Learn to understand the mind, body and spirit connection
to your health and well-being and how to
release disrupted or stuck energy

Be given insight into how your thoughts develop into your words
and those words become your actions,
those actions will eventually become your habits and
your habits will eventually constitute who you become

Identify powerful self-healing techniques that you can
use each and every day in The Healing Garden

Discover what lower vibrating energies are, how to release
them, leaving you feeling healthy with a positive well-being

Learn that perfect health is your divine right and how
manifesting perfect health becomes second nature to you

Discover amazing tools and techniques to find who,
where and what are your energy drainers
and how to quickly eliminate them.

Handbook   CD   Journal

The Dreams and Aspirations Garden

Relates to your dreams and aspirations, this garden will show you not just how to raise them but also how to achieve them.

Be guided into making firm decisions within your mind
to what your Dreams and Aspirations truly are
and pledge firmly that you will achieve them

Be guided to achieve the Dreams and Aspirations that
you are aiming towards with a positive mindset and true belief

Turn your Dreams and Aspirations into a firm plan of action
breaking down each Dream and Aspiration
into manageable steps to achieve them

Be excited with vast enthusiasm, courage and pride
as your creativity juices will be flowing beyond belief
because you will know that your Dreams and Aspirations
are definitely achievable!

Become a co-creator with the powers of your subconscious
mind who is your faithful Dreams or Aspirations Genie.
You will discover the magic of his powers
to creating an amazing life

Handbook   CD   Journal

The Angel Garden

Relates to your Angelic realm.
This Garden will show you how to open the door to communicating with The Angels; enabling you to start on a magnificent journey of enlightenment.

The Angels will offer answers for you to achieve your desires

The Angels will determine ways of solving any dilemmas or troubles you may be experiencing

The Angels will offer to you assistance and direction to whatever questions you may ask them

The Angelic Realm opens the portal to many miracles in your life

The Angels show you how to become open and receptive to Grace Energy in your life

The Angels will offer assistance to develop your career, family and relationships

Handbook	CD	Journal

The Forgiveness Garden

Relates to you removing the shackles of un-forgiveness, enabling you to live a life of freedom and joy

Discover the tools to release the control and power the other person and situation has over you by offering true forgiveness

Discover faith, trust and security to move beyond the unbearable sequence of un-forgiveness

Learn how to work with the forgiveness wheel

Learn how to work with the magic of time.
Time is a great healer and retreating into
The Forgiveness Garden offers you
magical positive outcomes you wish for and deserve

Learn how to not allow this to happen again in the future
by making decisions in life to forgive instantly
and take the relevant actions to forgive and create peace
and space for good things in life to move in

When you decide that you wish to forgive
you have to make a stronger commitment to yourself
for a course of action for change.

Handbook　　　　　CD　　　　　Journal

The Releasing and Letting Go Garden

Relates to you releasing and letting go of all negativity from your mind, body and soul; allowing you to live a healthy, happy and abundant life.

Release and let go of negative feelings allowing you to move
forward in life without the baggage that holds you back

Release and let go the feelings of hurt and anger
that stop you from forgiving

When you do not release and let go
you encounter unproductive and self-destructive feelings
that literally take over your life

By releasing and letting go a transformation within your mind,
body and spirit occurs; you feel free and finally at peace

Understand a feeling is just a feeling that needs
to be felt and released.

Releasing and letting go will restore faith
in you to be bigger than the conflict

Handbook   CD   Journal

The Fountain of Youth Garden

Relates to you transforming your mind, body and spirit by rejuvenating your energy on all levels.
In this garden you will learn how to enhance your youthfulness and revive your spiritual essence.

Live a healthy and optimistic lifestyle, giving you a longer life and greater well-being

Aspire to live a healthy, balanced life

Think, live and breathe health in your body, in your mind, in your finances and in your relationships

Discover the real you as a splendid, unique being with boundless potential and aptitude for experiencing the beauty and love of yourself and extending love to others

View the world in all of its full shining glory and live, laugh love with gushing youthful energy

Understand the highest importance of power of the subconscious mind and consciously fuel it with positive thoughts

Understand that having an optimistic attitude to change decreases the progression of physical ageing in the body

Handbook   CD   Journal

The Crystal Garden

Relates to you bringing harmony to your mind, body and spirit through the use of crystals.
Working on the subtle layers and chakras you will discover your connection to Mother Earth; learning to channel unwanted energies back to her for recycling.

How to connect with your crystals and attune them to your mind becoming one with your consciousness

How to discover to combine various crystals for health, wealth and abundance

A technique that will reinforce your connection to the earth and convey a stronger flow of earth energies that will enhance mind, body and spirit

How to combine your personal energy with that of gem stones for self healing and self love

How to make a Crystal Manifesting Box to manifest all that you wish for in life

How to make your personal Crystal Grid to enhance all aspects of your life.

Handbook   **CD**   **Journal**

The Gratitude Garden

Relates to having or not having gratitude in your life.
It will show you how to be grateful for everyone and everything in your life; which then brings you more things to be grateful for.

How to discover your personal Gratitude Manifesting Box.
Your Gratitude Manifesting Box will draw to you
more things to be grateful for

'The Attitude of Gratitude' which will make a huge impact
on your life and well-being

How to achieve a state of pure unadulterated BLESSEDNESS
in The Gratitude Garden, making gratitude
your natural state of being

How discovering a grateful state of mind will draw to you
the people, circumstances and events that your heart desires.

How to plant Gratitude seeds on your
personal Gratitude seed map

How you will discover the silver chord, achieving
and receiving pure gratefulness in life.

Handbook　　　　CD　　　　Journal

Lightning Source UK Ltd.
Milton Keynes UK
UKOW031333170112

185555UK00011B/33/P